GERHARD GRAF-MARTINEZ

Flamenco

GUITAR METHOD

VOLUME 2
FOR TEACHING AND PRIVATE STUDY
STANDARD MUSIC NOTATION & TABLATURE

ED 9395

SCHOTT
Mainz · London · Madrid · New York · Paris · Prag · Tokyo · Toronto

ED 9395
ISMN M-001-13110-0
ISBN 3-7957-5582-4

© 2003 Schott Musik International, Mainz

Cover photo: Claudia Ammann
Photos:
Elke Stolzenberg (Madrid)
Günther Paust (Waiblingen)
Katrin Schandner (Frankfurt)
Hardy Edelmann (Zürich)
Walter Mauritz (Wien)
Layout und Music Typography:
MusikDesign Gerhard Graf-Martinez, Schorndorf

Translated by Heike Brühl

Printed in Germany · BSS 50507
www.schott-music.com

Contents

List of Compositions and Music Examples 4

Lesson 6   6

    Arpegio 9
    Tremolo 22

Lesson 7   27

    Picado 29

Lesson 8   37

    Bulerías I 39

Lesson 9   55

    Alzapúa 57

Lesson 10   63

    Soleá 65
    Alegrías 70
    Bulerías II 81
    Tarantos 86
    Tangos 86

Estilos   93

    Estilos 95

History   113

    Introduction 115
    Antiquity 115
    Middle Ages 117
    The Moors 118
    The Reconquista 120
    The Jews 120
    The Inquisition 121
    The Conquista 122
    The Gipsies 122
    Terminology 124
    Development of Flamenco 126
    Flamenco in the 50s and Today 127
    Los Tablaos 127
    El Cante - El Baile - El Toque 128
    Pasión 128
    Bibliography 129
    Epilogue 130
    CD Tracks 131
    Index 133

List of Music Examples and Compositions

Arpegio Exercise I 9
Arpegio Exercise II 9
Arpegio Exercise III 10
Arpegio Exercise IV 10
Quejío II (Taranto) 11
Mantón IV (Soleá) 13
Mantón V (Soleá 15
Mantón VI (Soleá) 17
Rumbita II (Rumba) 19
Tremolo Exercise I 22
Tremolo Exercise II 23
Quejío III (Taranto) 24
Picado Exercise I 30
Picado Exercise II 30
Picado Exercise III 30
Mi-Dórico 31
La-Dórico 31
Si-Dórico 31

Fa#-Dórico 31

Lérida (Garrotin) 32
Compás Exercise I (Bulerías) 40
Compás Exercise II (Bulerías) 40
Compás Exercise III (Bulerías) 40
Compás Exercise IV (Bulerías) 40
Bulerías-Compás I 41
Bulerías-Compás II 41
Bulerías-Compás III 42
Bulerías-Compás IV 42
Bulerías-Compás V 43
Bulerías-Compás VI 43
Bulerías-Compás VII 43
Bulerías-Compás VIII 44
Bulerías-Compás IX 44
Bulerías-Compás X 44
Bulerías-Compás XI 45
Bulerías-Compás XII 45
Bulerías-Compás XIII 46
Bulerías-Compás XIV 46
Bulerías-Compás XV 47
Bulerías-Compás XVI 47
Bulerías-Compás XVII 47
Bulerías-Compás XVIII 48
Columpio I (Bulerías) 49
Columpio II (Bulerías) 51
Columpio III (Bulerías) 52
Alzapúa I (Exercise) 58
Alzapúa II (Exercise) 58
Alzapúa III (Exercise) 59
Alzapúa IV (Bulerías) 59
Alzapúa V (Bulerías) 61
Alzapúa VI (Bulerías) 61

Mantón VIII (Soleá)	65
Mantón IX (Soleá)	66
Mantón X (Soleá)	67
Mantón XI (Soleá)	68
Alegría en Mi I (Compás Exercise)	70
Alegría en Mi II (Compás Exercise)	71
Alegría en Mi III (Intro)	73
Alegría en Mi IV (Escobilla)	74
Alegría en Mi V (Puente)	75
Caí II (Alegría en Do)	76
Caí III (Alegría en Do)	77
Caí IV (Alegría en Do)	79
Caí V (Alegría en Do)	80
Columpio IV (Bulerías Intro)	81
Columpio V (Bulerías)	85
Quejío IV (Taranto)	86
Naino VI (Tangos)	89
Naino VII (Tangos)	91
Naino VIII (Tangos)	92

CD cover of MODO NUEVO Gerhard Graf-Martinez (Boulevard-Records)   Photo: Günter Paust

LESSON 6

- **Arpegio**
- **Quejío II (Taranto)**
- **Mantón IV (Soleá)**
- **Mantón V (Soleá)**
- **Mantón VI (Soleá)**
- **Rumbita II (Rumba)**
- **Tremolo**
- **Tremolo-Exercise I**
- **Tremolo-Exercise II**
- **Quejío III (Taranto)**

Enrique de Melchor and Gerhard Graf-Martinez (1983) Photo: Walter Mauritz

Arpegio

When playing *arpegio* (arpeggio) the thumb is always played *apoyando,* unless the adjacent string is struck with, say, *i* simultaneously or immediately afterwards. **Arpegio Exercises I-IV** are purely technical exercises, aimed at coordinating both hands or serving as "warm-ups".

Strike close to the bridge

Arpegio-Exercise I

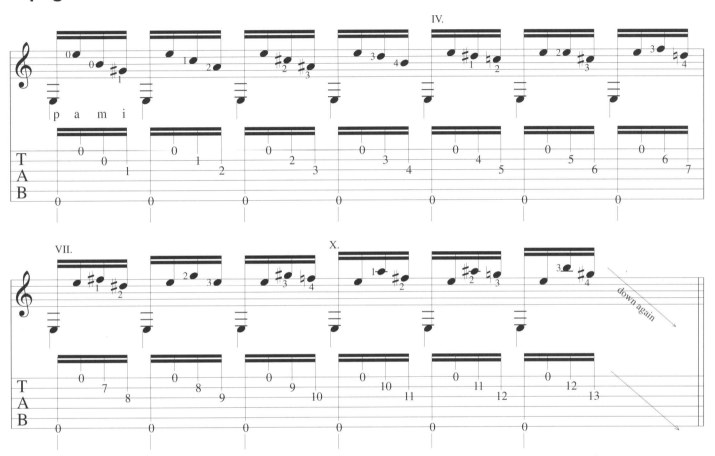

Arpegio-Exercise II

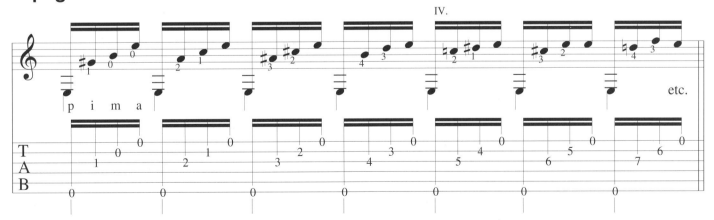

Arpegio Exercises I and **II** should also be practised with *p-m-i-a, p-m-a-i, p-a-i-m* and *p-i-a-m* as well as with *i-p-m-a* and *a-p-m-i*.

LESSON 6

Arpegio-Exercise III

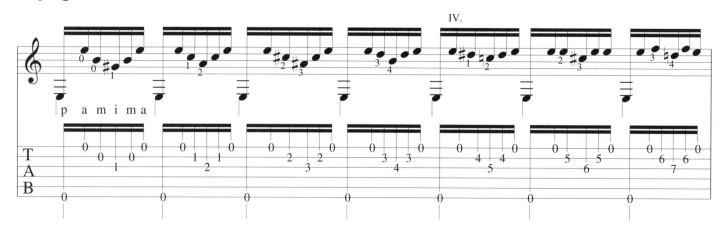

Arpegio-Exercise IV

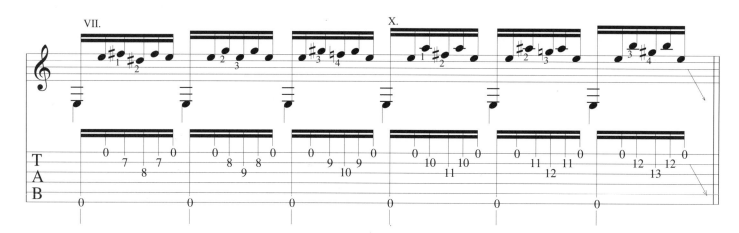

p always *apoyando*

SABICAS, too, used to play this *arpegio* in **Exercise IV** beginning with *p-i-m-a,* but then pulled his ring finger back across the treble strings. It's incredible – and you can hear his wonderful arpegio on countless recordings.

To achieve a beautiful *arpegio,* you shouldn't only practise the examples shown in this book, but also the classical ones such as the following: *p-i-m-i-a-i-m-i, p-a-m-a-i-a-m-a, p-m-i-m-p-a-m-i* and *p-i-m-a-i-m-a-i.*

The triplet arpegio is very commonly used. It sounds very nice if the bass note at the beginning is anticipated a little, i.e. *a* strikes shortly after *p*. In addition, these two notes, indicated by the pause (fermata), are held a little longer.

To play the pulled-back *a*-arpegio fluently, indicated by the wavy line, *p, i, m* and *a* should be placed on the strings before the stroke. After striking with *p, i* and *m*, *a* is played across all strings from ① to ⑥.

Regarding the chords played across the strings with *p*, I would like to emphasise again that the forearm doesn't move downwards, but is only turned, because otherwise the fingers will lose their orientation.

Quejío II (Taranto)

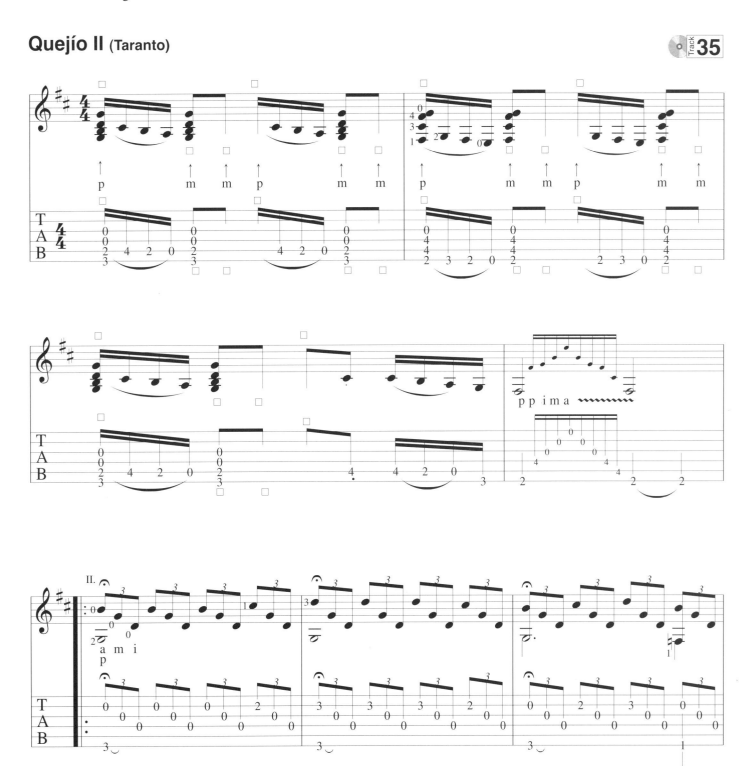

LESSON 6

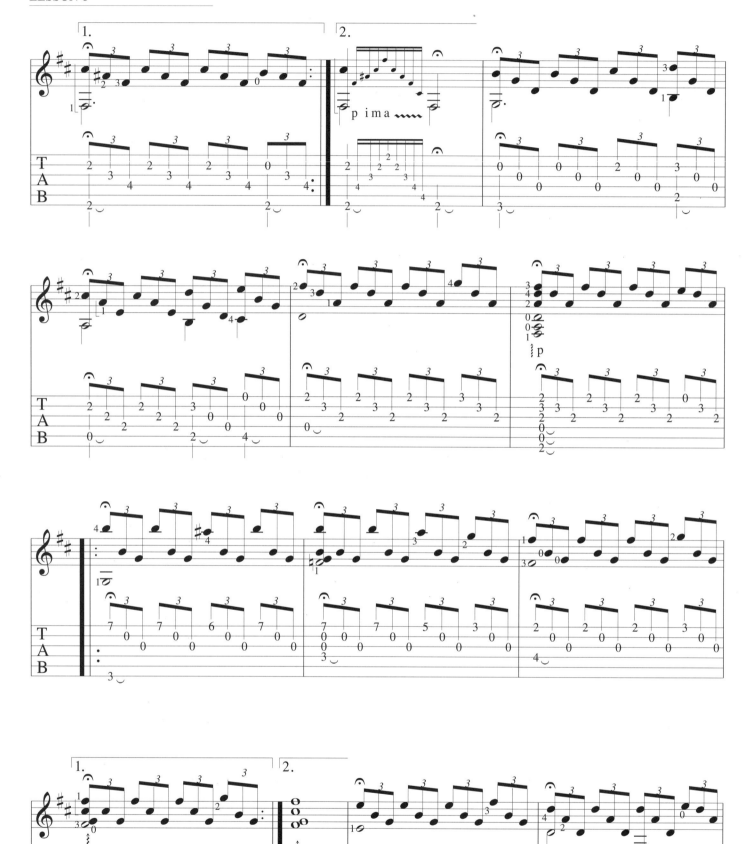

Arpegio

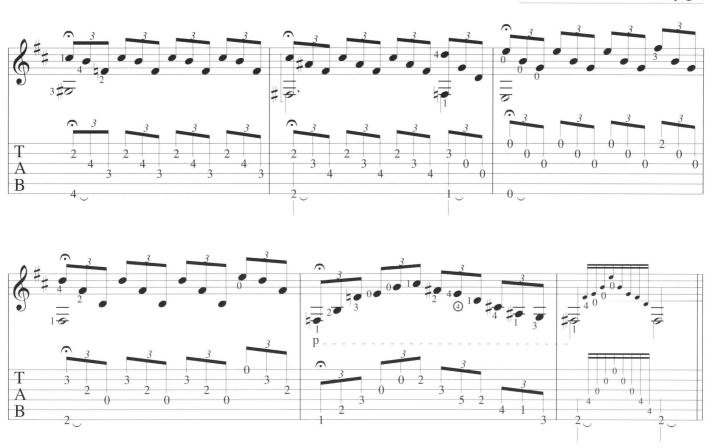

In lines 1 and 5 of **Mantón IV** (Soleá) it is again advisable to place *a*, *m* and *i* on their respective strings before playing the triplet appoggiaturas. The arpeggiated downstrokes with *p* should not be played too fast.

The sixteenth (semiquaver) sextuplets in lines 2 and 4 should be played very slowly at first, so they will sound much more sophisticated when played at a faster tempo later.

I'd particularly like to point out the eighth-note (quaver) triplets in line 4 which are easily overlooked or not played at the correct tempo. All subsequent single notes are played with *p*.

Mantón IV (Soleá)

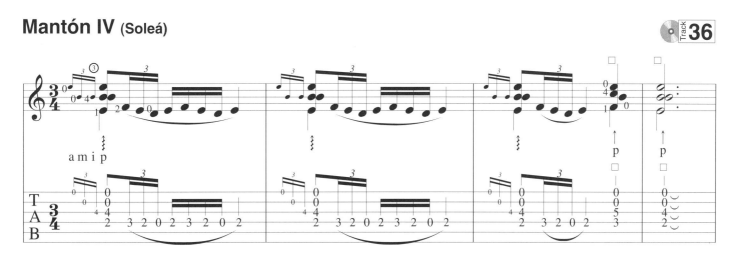

LESSON 6

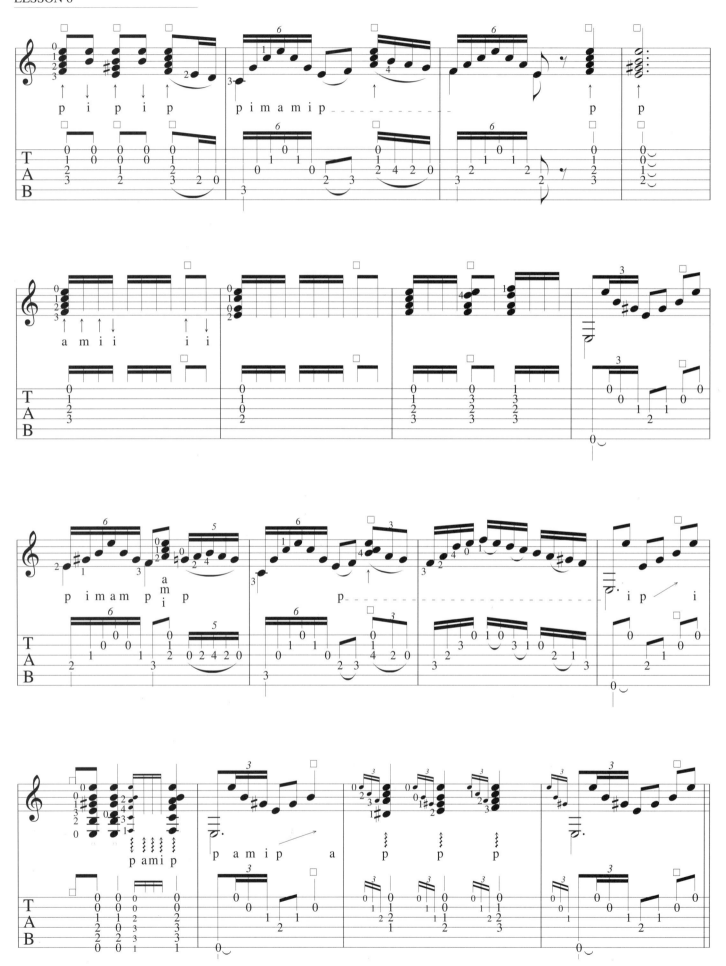

Lines 2 and 3 or 4 and 5, respectively, of **Mantón V** (Soleá) may also be used to accompany the third and fourth *tercio* in the *cante* (see **Estilos**). When playing the tied F chord in the first bar of the second line, you will get the correct note value if you imagine a *golpe* on beat 4, or actually execute a golpe when starting.

Mantón VI (Soleá) is supposed to show how a *falseta* may be varied. The five variations are based on the same theme.

Mantón V (Soleá)

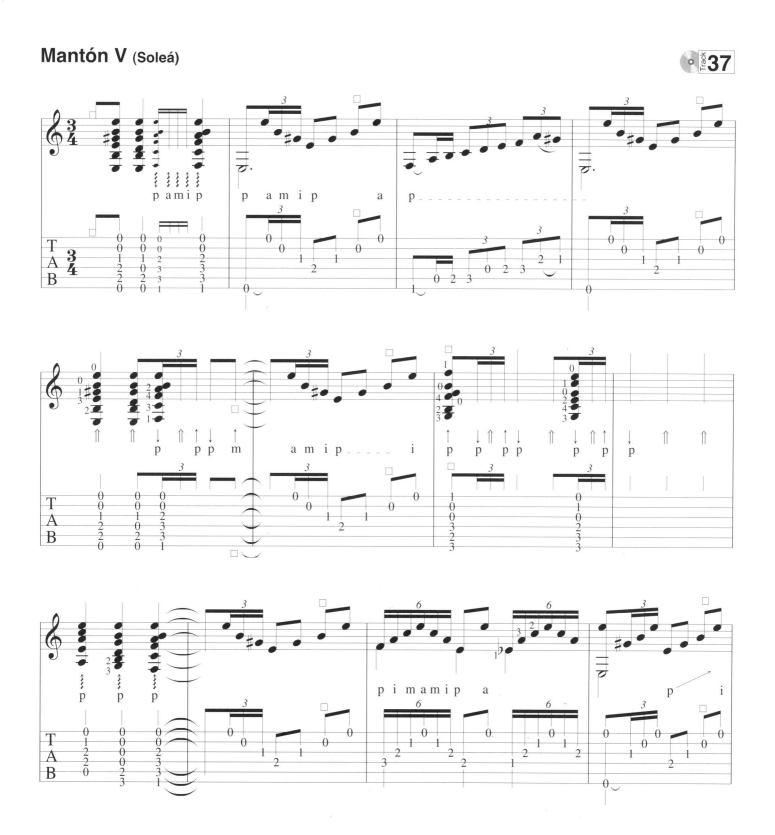

LESSON 6

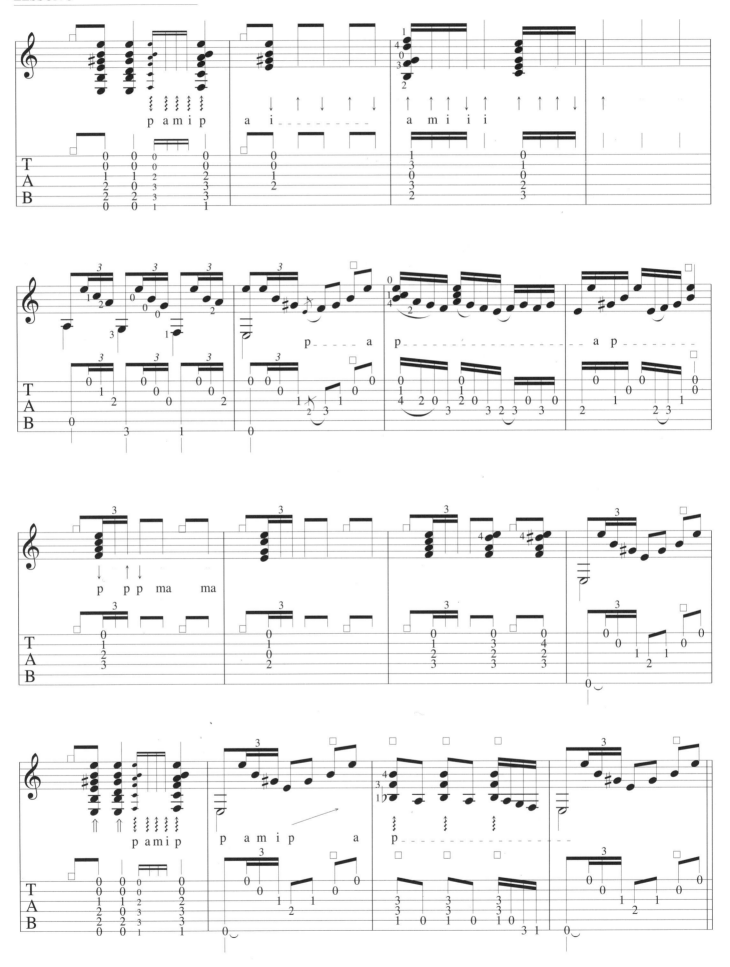

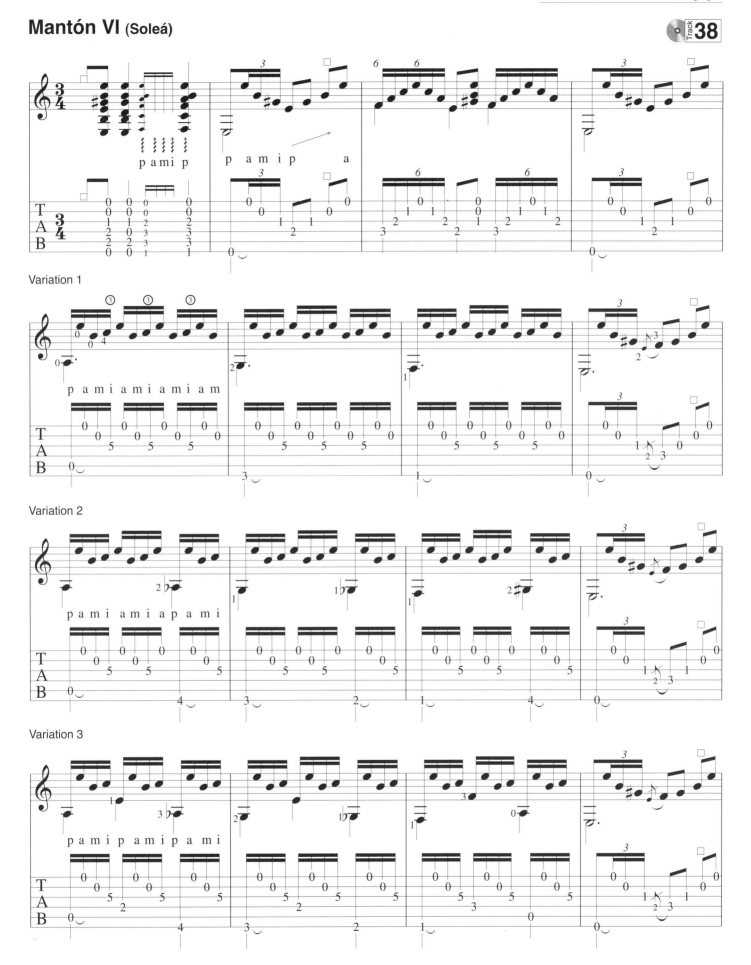

LESSON 6

Variation 4

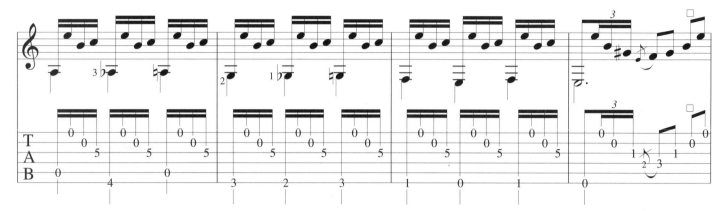

Variation 5

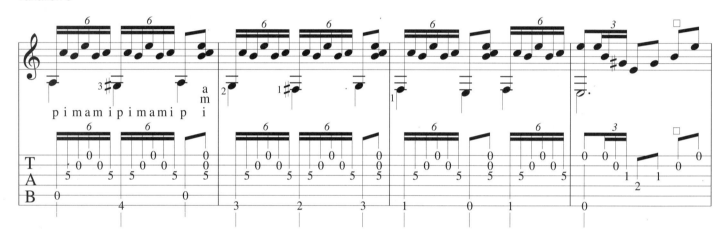

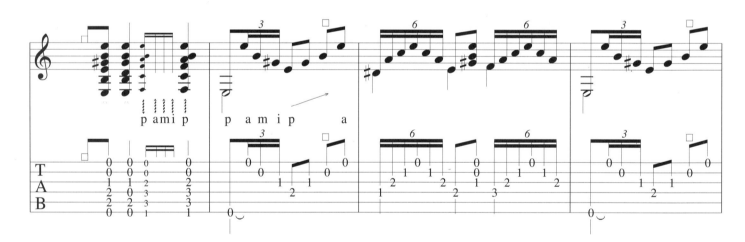

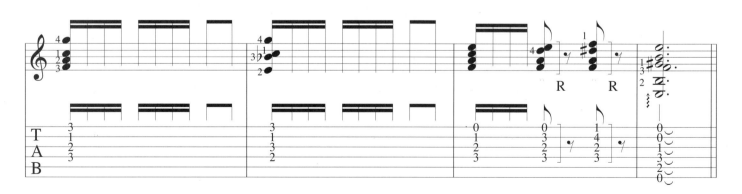

Rumbita II (Rumba)

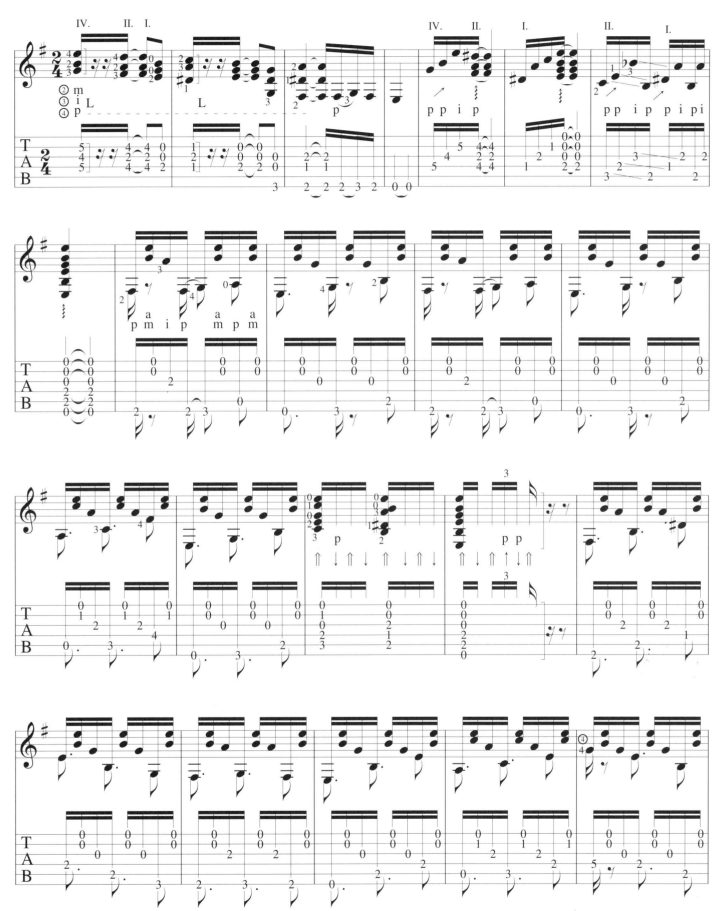

LESSON 6

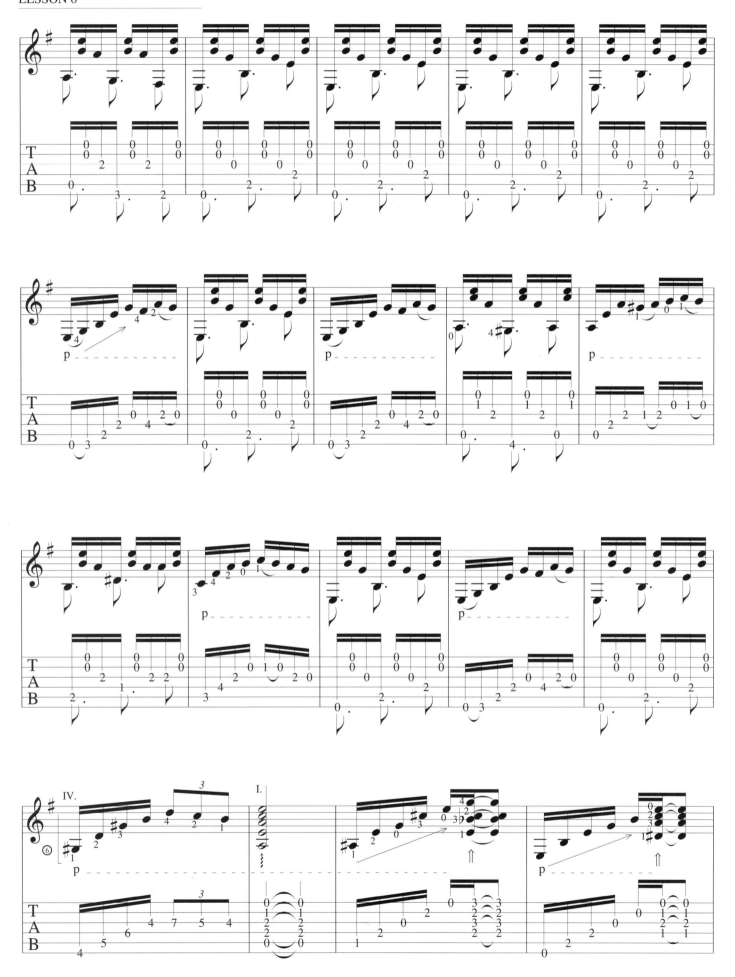

Arpegio

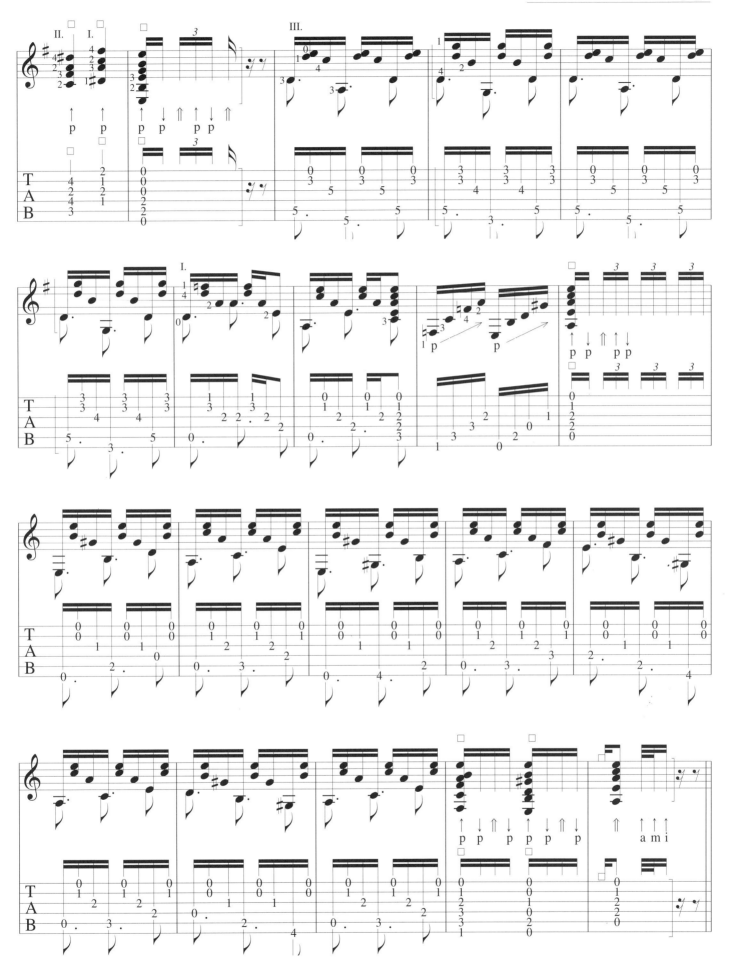

Tremolo

The traditional Flamenco tremolo is played in a quintuplet. The sequence is *p-i-a-m-i*, the thumb is again placed on the string *(apoyando)*. All finger combinations of Tremolo **Exercise I** should be practised for a while to make the *tremolo* sound nice and round.

Tremolo Exercise I

1.) p i a m i
2.) p m a m i
3.) p i m a m

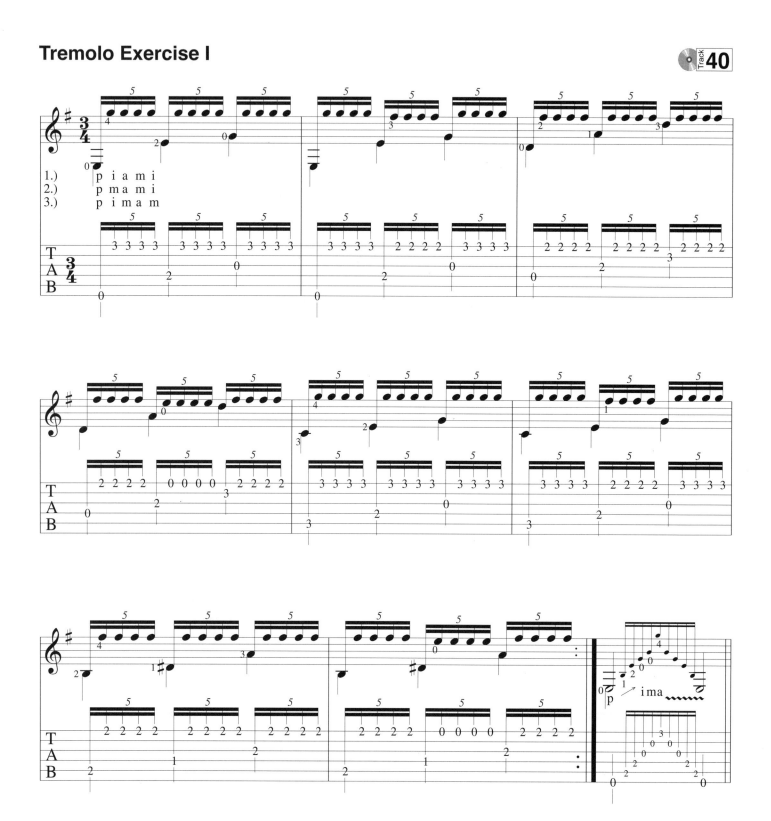

Tremolo

Today, the tremolo is not only played in quintuplets, but also in countless variations. Sixtuplets, septuplets etc. are often used. Mostly, the bass note is anticipated a little or is played simultaneously with the top part (e.g. with *i*). Or, the first note of the bar, indicated by a pause, is sustained longer than the other bass notes.

Tremolo Exercise II

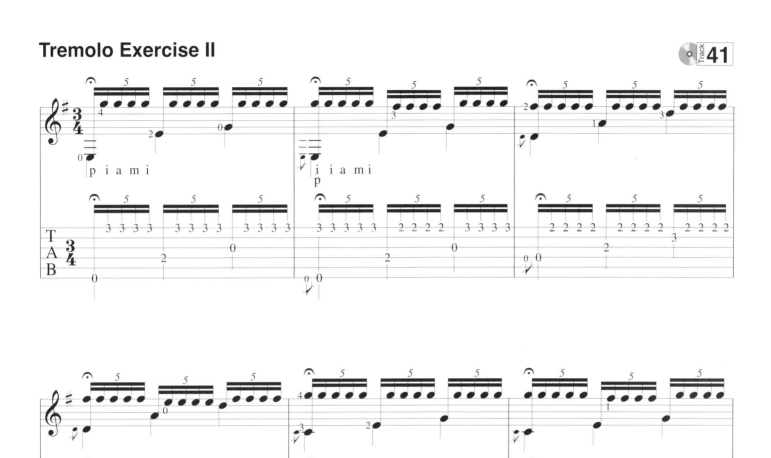

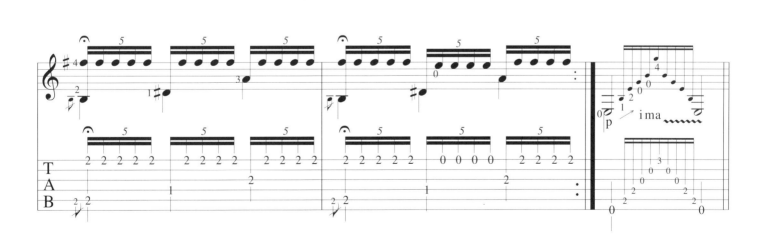

23

LESSON 6

The tremolo in **Quejío III** (Taranto) includes everything: a normal quintuplet tremolo, appoggiatura and pause. However, this example is not representative of all tremolos, for there are many more possibilities. It wouldn't make sense to dictate when or when not to play, say, an appoggiatura, because everything is played intuitively once you have mastered the technique. This tremolo only serves as an example – there is no limit to your own creativity and interpretation. From line 3, the simplified notation is used for the tremolo, i.e. the tremolo is continued as in line 2.

Tremolo

LESSON 6

LESSON 7

- Picado
- Picado Exercise I - III
- Mi-Dórico
- La-Dórico
- Si-Dórico
- Fa#-Dorico
- Lérida (Garrotin)

El Agujetas — Photo: Elke Stolzenberg

Picado

Paco de Lucía's picado technique has become a standard technique of the young *tocaores*. The old master Sabicas used it as well, but Paco's *picado* was even more sparkling and brilliant, and he played it with incredible velocity.

The brilliance and velocity are achieved merely by the postion of the hand. In this technique, the thumb is always placed on ⑥, except when ⑥ is played. By placing *p* on the string, the hand remains steady and can strike harder. The only source of the movement is the middle joint, never the large joint. You may well straighten and tense the large joint (knuckle) a little too much at the beginning to get used to holding your hand like this (see picture 7.1). As for the sequence of movements: the fingertip is placed on the string to be played (see picture 7.1). Now this string is pushed against the string below it, in this case ②, or, better, pushed towards the *tapa* (see picture 7.3). Due to the pressure, the fingertip, or, rather, the nail rolls off across the string and is placed on the next string (picture 7.2). Some guitarists don't straighten the tip joint, but nevertheless execute the stroke by using the middle joint as the source of movement.

If you are used to executing the alternating stroke with the large joint as the source of movement, it seems to be almost impossible to play this stroke. After some time, however, if you really keep straightening the hand at the large joint, this stroke, too, will become the most natural thing in the world. If necessary, you can check your movements with the help of a mirror.

This is the only stroke which creates the typical Flamenco picado which has become a standard. If it is played differently – it's just not Flamenco.

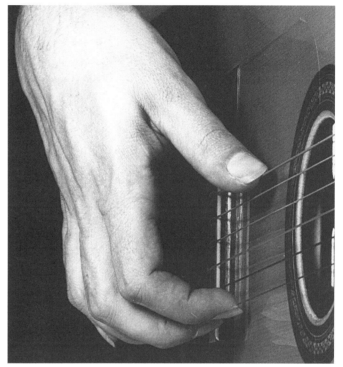

Picture 7.1

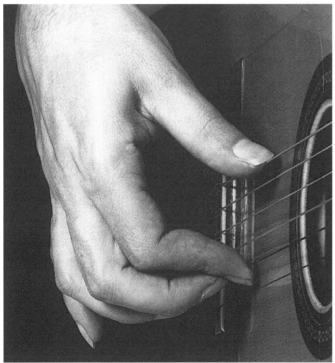

Picture 7.2

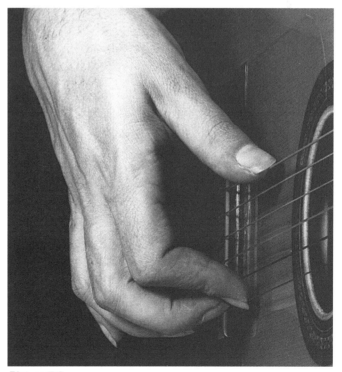

Picture 7.3

LESSON 7

The following exercises should be played as a daily warm-up. In these exercises, too, every movement should be executed slowly and consciously. The progressions *m-i* and *i-m* should not be played alternately, but should be practised separately.

Picado Exercise I

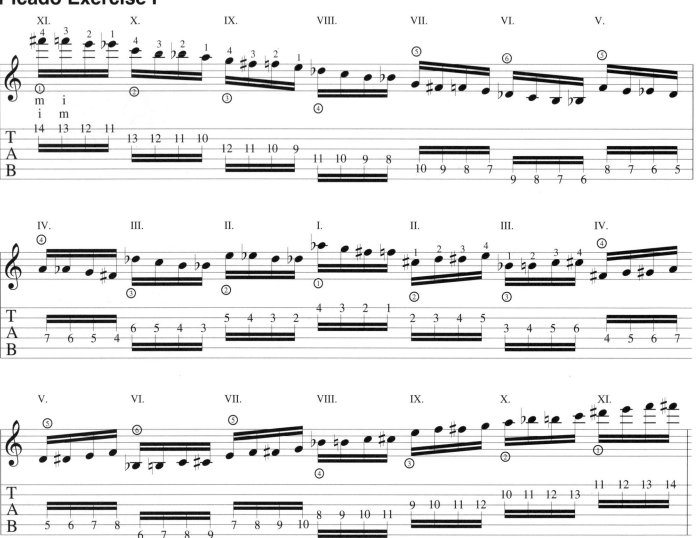

Picado Exercise II is the same as I, except that each note is struck twice, and in **Picado Exercise III** each note is played three times.

Picado Exercise II

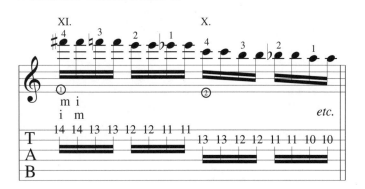

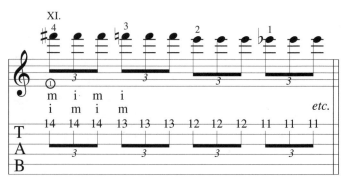

Picado

Here are the four most important scales in the Flamenco mode. This mode is called *modo dórico*. The notes with an accidental in parentheses are only played on the basic chord (the dominant). See **Volume I, Modo Dórico.**

Mi-Dórico

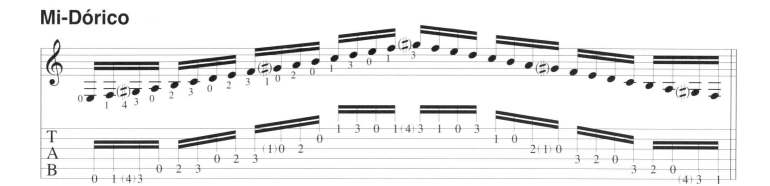

La-Dórico

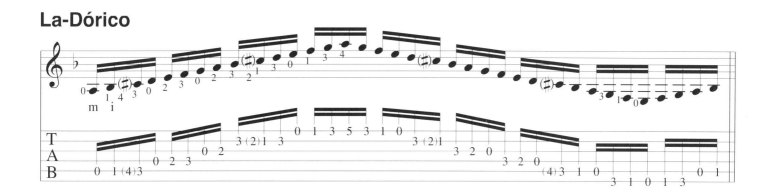

Si-Dórico

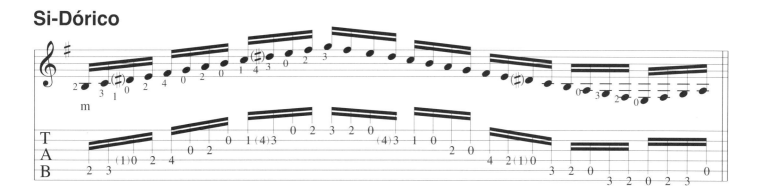

Fa♯-Dórico

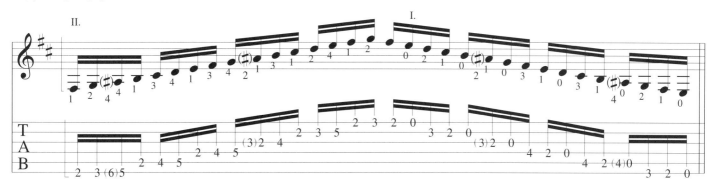

LESSON 7

In **Lérida** (Garrotin), the *picado* is combined with other techniques. The **Intro** doesn't require much explanation. The *p-i-m-a arpegio,* indicated by ⇑, sounds similar to the *p arpegio*.

In **Falseta 1**, the *picado* is combined with the *arpegio*. Make sure that the last three sixteenth notes (semiquavers) in the bar are really played *apoyando*. In the penultimate line the transition from *i-m-p* to *p* may also be played on the G in the second bar. It might take you a long time to learn this transition, because the position of the hand must be changed very quickly.

In **Falseta 2**, the *picado* is combined with a ⇑-downstroke. After the downstroke, when the fingers are below the strings, *p* should be placed on ⑥ immediately so that the hand is set for the *picado*.

In the last line of **Falseta 3**, the *picado* is combined with a p-downstroke.

Lérida (Garrotin)

Intro

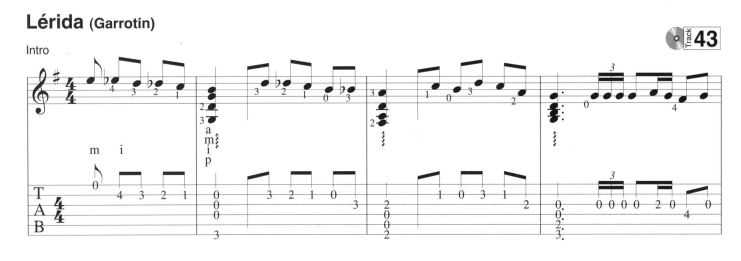

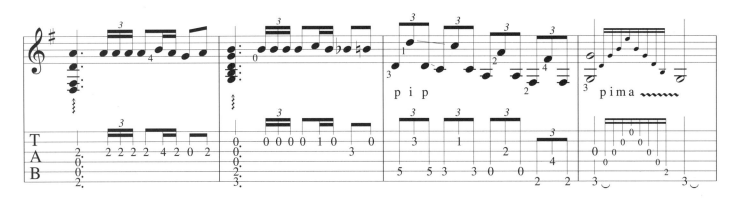

Falseta 1

Picado

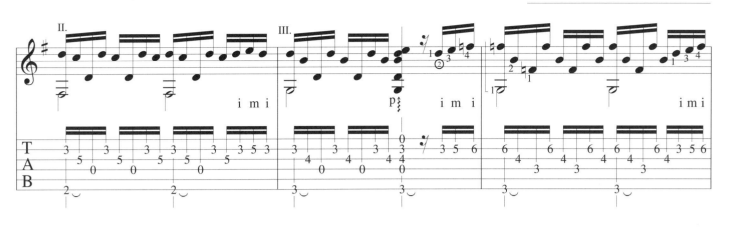
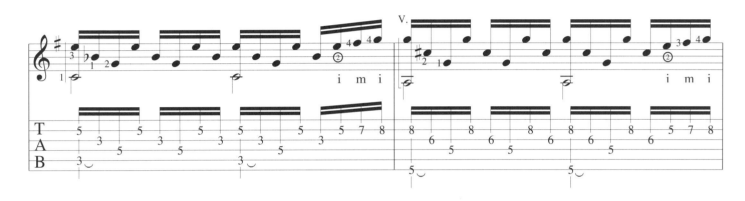
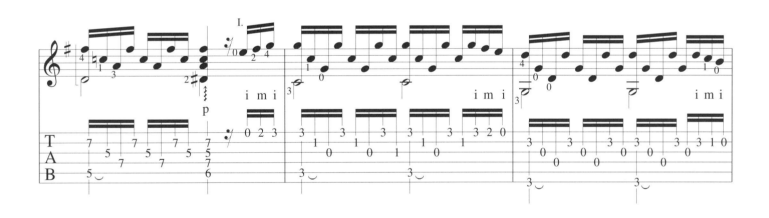
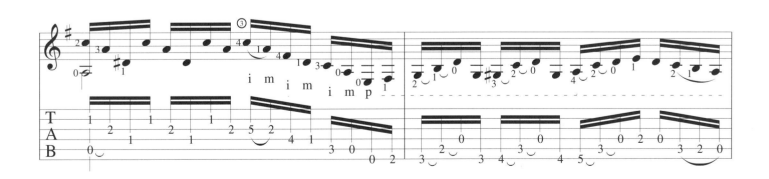

LESSON 7

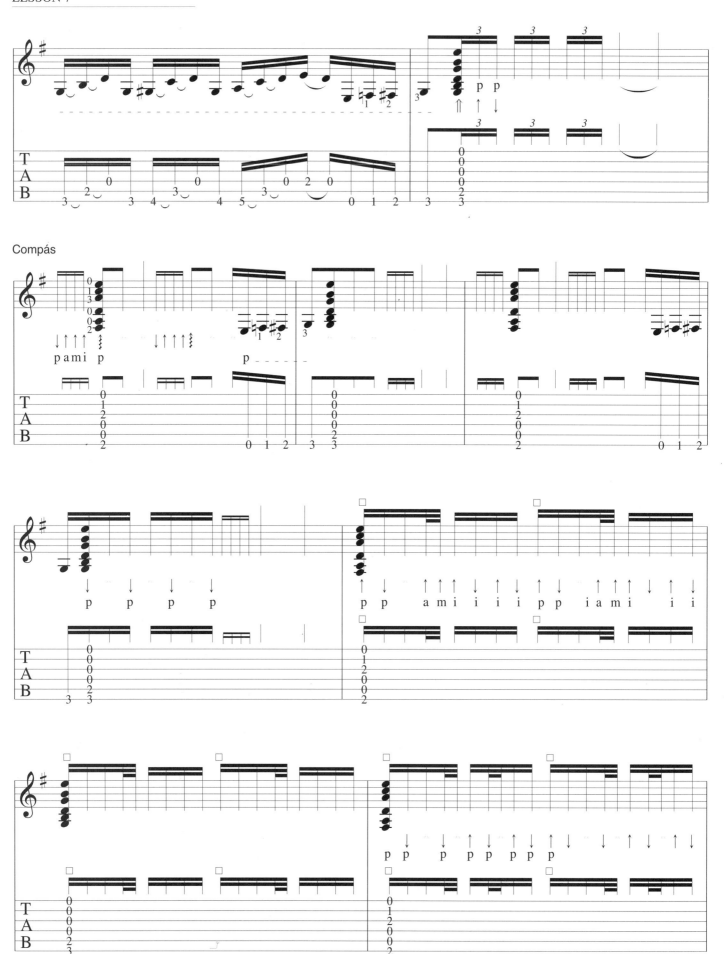

Compás

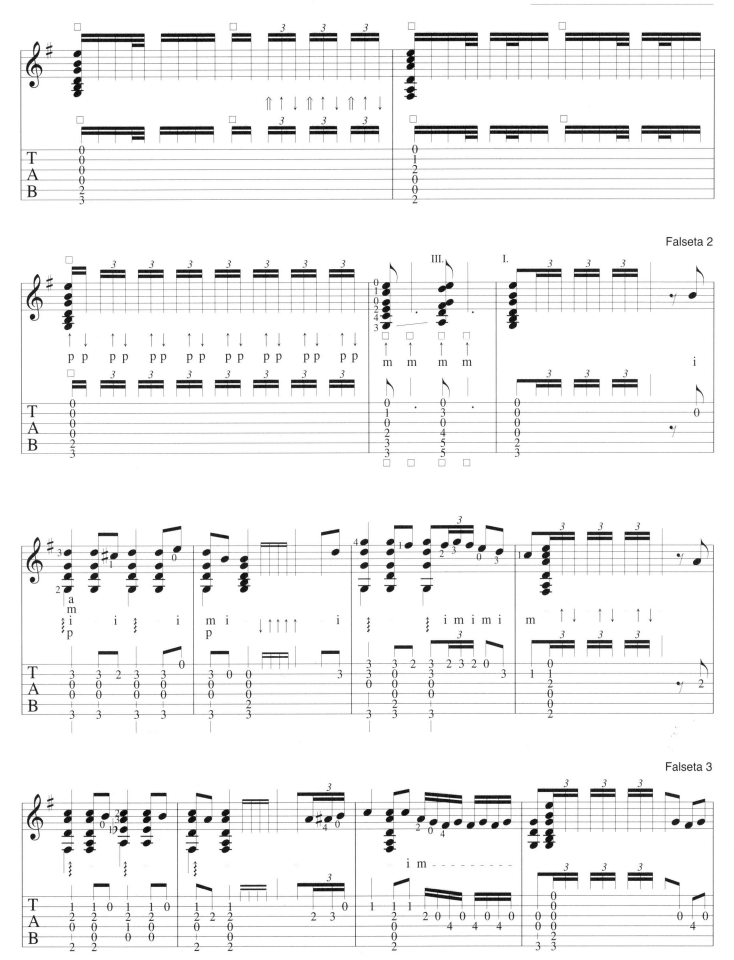

LESSON 7

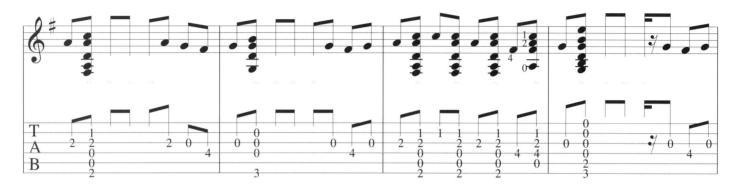

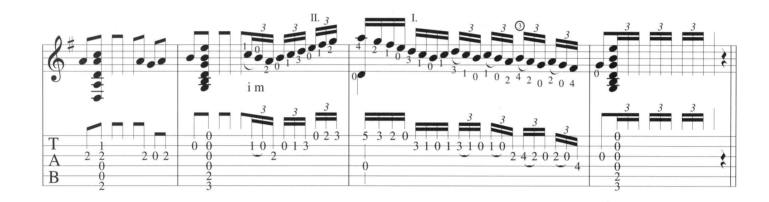

Paco de Lucía, Andrés Batista and Gerhard Graf-Martinez

LESSON 8

- **Bulerías I**
- **Compás Exercise I-IV (Bulerías)**
- **Bulerías-Compás I - XVIII**
- **La Horquilla**
- **Columpio I (Bulerías)**
- **Columpio II (Bulerías)**
- **Pregunta Respuesta Desarrollo**
- **Columpio III (Bulerías)**

El Cabrero

Photo: Hardy Edelmann

Bulerías I

The **Bulerías** belong to the most popular toques, especially for the young guitarists, because *compás* security and virtuosity can be shown to their best advantage. Experience shows that if you fully understand the *compás* of the **Bulerías** and its variations, you will find the rhythms of the other *estilos,* played according to the 12-beat *compás,* easier. Even though some guitarists play them very gently or "academically," the **Bulería** is and will always be the Flamenco style which is played very powerfully, especially by the *gitanos.* Not only in *toque,* but also in *cante* and *baile.* Whereas solos are mostly played in "La-dórico," you will find all kinds of modes in the acompañamiento. To a good *tocaor* that means he should also be able to play the **Bulerías** in the major and minor modes, as well as *por arriba* (Mi-dórico). Often, other *estilos* are sung in the *compás* of the **Bulerías.** In this case they are called **Soleá por Bulerías,** "Fandango por Bulerías," "Taranto por Bulerías," to name just a few examples, and are transposed into a variety of keys. The sisters BERNARDA Y FERNANDA DE UTRERA are known for their skill to add any copla of any *palos* to the **Bulerías.** Together with SABICAS, CARMEN AMAYA adapted "Las dos puntas" (released on: Carmen Amaya – Le Chant du Monde, LDX 74880) during her South America tour. A record by PACO DE LUCIA, released in Japan, includes a **Bulería** called " Huida" in Sol#-dórico. The AMADOR brothers, better known as "Pata Negra," play **Bulerías** over a blues cadence on their record "Blues de la Frontera" (Nuevos Medios). I could list many more examples to show the wealth of variations of the **Bulerías.**

The *compás* is not so difficult if you count correctly. Many players count

1 · 2 · 3 · 4 · 5 · 6 · 7 · 8 · 9 · 10 · 11 · 12,

which you will also find in most guitar methods. Someone invented this way of counting a long time ago, and many others just copied it without questioning it. It is not really wrong, but it isn't the best way either, because on the one hand, most *coplas* and *falsetas* don't start on the 1, and, on the other hand, because beginners find it very difficult to hear the *compás* or to count along, let alone the fact that it will take very long to understand the **Bulerías** if you use this way of counting. It is much easier to start on the accented *12* and to notate the whole thing with alternating time signatures.

⁶/₈   *1 · 2 · 3 · 4 · 5 · 6*   ³/₄   *1 · and · 2 · and · 3 · and*

The accents are the same, but the sense of time is completely different or, rather, it has just begun to exist. In ⁶/₈ time, the *12* is the *1* and the *3* is the *4*, in ³/₄ time, the *6* is the *1*, the *8* is the *2* and the *10* is the *3*.

Clock ⁶/₈   *12 · 1 · 2 · 3 · 4 · 5*   ³/₄   *6 · 7 · 8 · 9 · 10 · 11*

Time ⁶/₈   *1 · 2 · 3 · 4 · 5 · 6*   ³/₄   *1 · and · 2 · and · 3 · and*

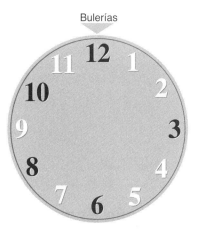

Before you begin with the *compás* exercises on your guitar, you should practise the following four examples with a metronome until you can accompany simple **Bulerías** on records or on the enclosed CD with palmas. This kind of percussive accompaniment is also part of the jaleo and should be the most natural thing in the world for every *tocaor.*

The percussion notes above the staff line are the *palmas* (see **Volume I**), the notes below are for the foot. The beats of the alternating ⁶/₈-³/₄ time are indicated above the staff, the beats of the Flamenco clock *(reloj)* below the staff. At this point, I'd like to mention that it is always advisable to move the foot when playing Flamenco guitar to check your " timing." Don't move it on the beats, but on the accents.

LESSON 8

Compás Exercise I:
The *falsetas* of the traditional **Bulerías** strictly kept to this basic form.

Compás Exercise I (Bulerías)

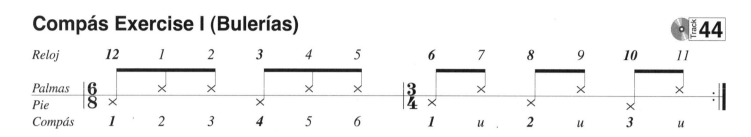

Compás Exercise II:
If you are accompanied by a bailaor or *jaleador* you will definitely hear this *compás*.

Compás Exercise II (Bulerías)

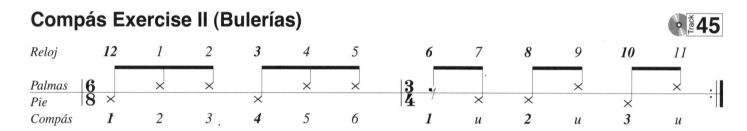

Compás Exercise III:
Here are the famous *contras* which are all the more difficult the faster they are played, especially if, in addition to playing, you have to tap the accents with your foot.

Compás Exercise III (Bulerías)

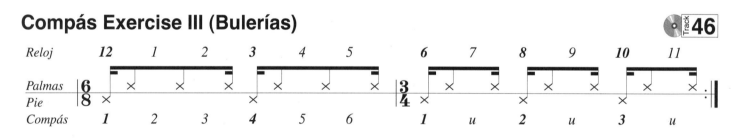

Compás Exercise IV:
The gitanos have a special kind of "swing" in their Bulerías, also called "como un caballo" (like a galloping horse). This compás doesn't really require alternating time signatures, since it is played in 3/4 time throughout. Many falsetas are played in this aire, or only in 6/8 time. More details are provided later.

Compás Exercise IV (Bulerías)

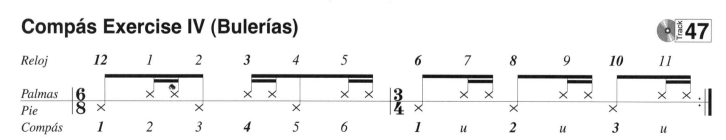

Bulerías-Compás I-IV are all played in the same rhythm. The only thing that varies is the accentuation with the foot *(pie)*. I deliberately included no chord changes because coordinating the right hand and the foot is difficult enough. If the apagado "]L" (left hand) causes problems, it can be left out at first so that the chords will ring.

Bulerías-Compás I:
The foot meticulously taps the accents: *12, 3, 6, 8, 10*. Make sure that the *rasgueo* in this exercise and the following exercises begins on *9* and ends on *10*. After the last upstroke with *p* (beat *10*), the thumb is immediately placed on ⑥ again.

Bulerías-Compás I

Track 48

Cejilla III

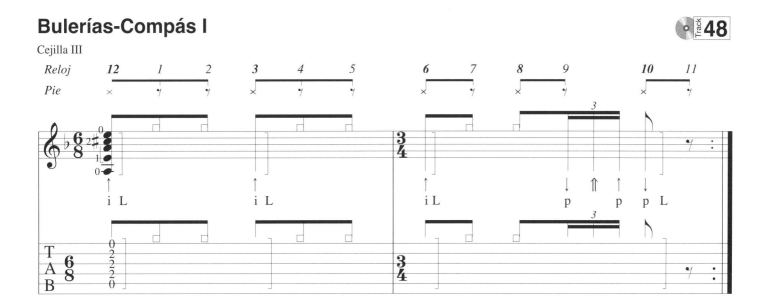

Bulerías-Compás II:
Many tocaores are using this kind of foot control. Since PACO DE LUCÍA also applies it as well, some guitarists use it to demonstrate their absolute mastery of the *compás*. If it has a negative impact on the aire, however, it will be better to use the foot of the **Bulerías-Compás I**. In this case it is impossible to fathom out if the *compás* ends in 6/8 or in 3/4 time.

Bulerías-Compás II:

Track 49

Cejilla III

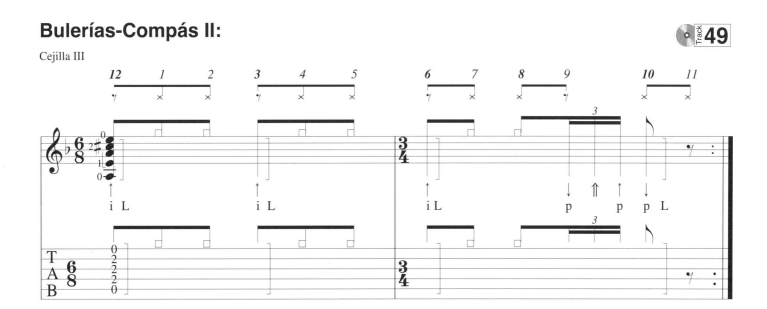

LESSON 8

Bulerías-Compás III:
This foot-compás is hardly ever used. It is very suitable as a rhythm exercise, however. Moreover, as I mentioned before, it is important to have this compás in your head.

Bulerías-Compás III:

Cejilla III

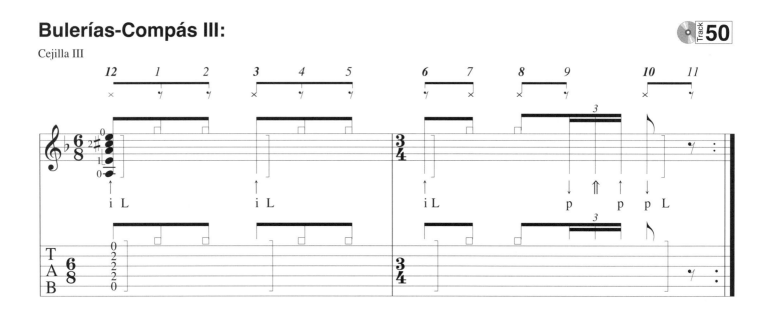

Bulerías-Compás IV:
You can already try this foot-accompaniment which is mainly used by the *gitanos*. However, don't use it as a basis for the Bulerías-compás until you have worked through this book, i.e. only if you feel secure with the "compás alterno" (alternating time).

Bulerías-Compás IV:

Cejilla III

Falseta 1

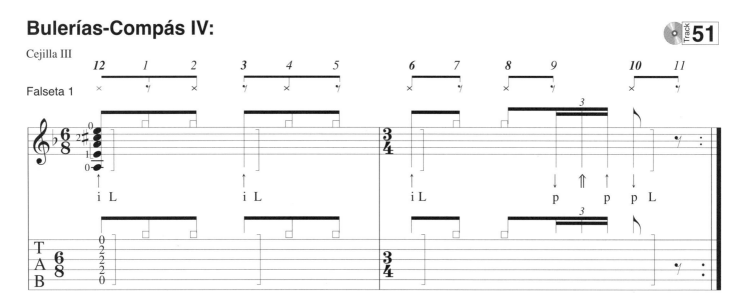

Bulerías-Compás V - X: should all be practised with the foot accentuation indicated above the staff. Try the foot accentuation indicated below the **Bulerías-Compás V** later.

Note the different *cierres* in each exercise. *Cierre* means end – in this case the *rasgueos* end on beat **10**.

Also notice if the *apagados* are played with the left or right hand.

Bulerías-Compás V

Cejilla III

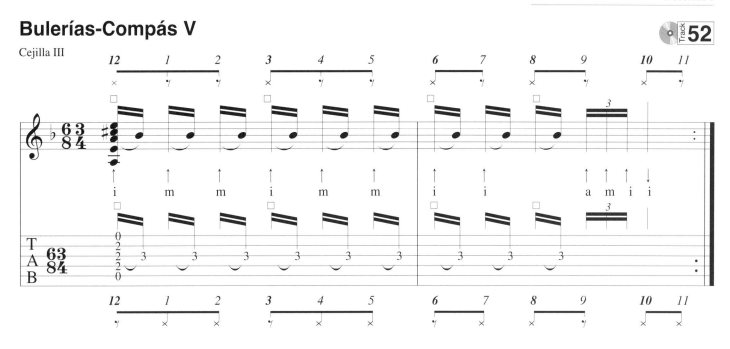

Bulerías-Compás VI

Cejilla III

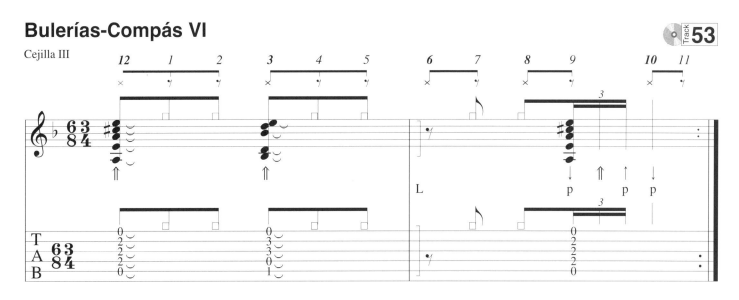

Bulerías-Compás VII

Cejilla III

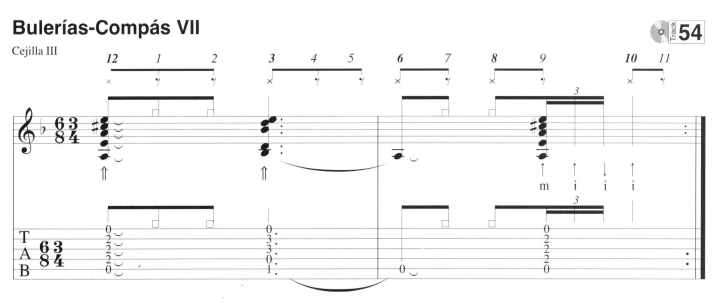

LESSON 8

Bulerías-Compás VIII

Cejilla III

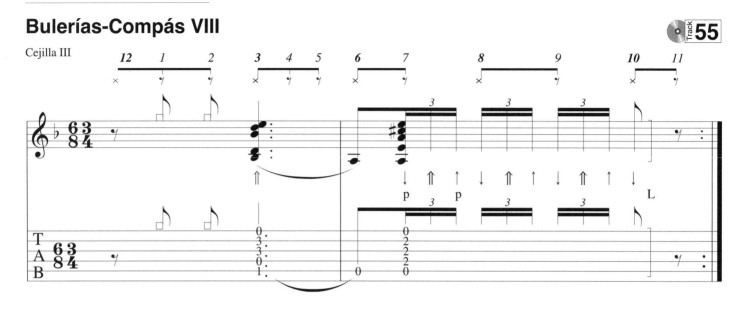

Bulerías-Compás IX

Cejilla III

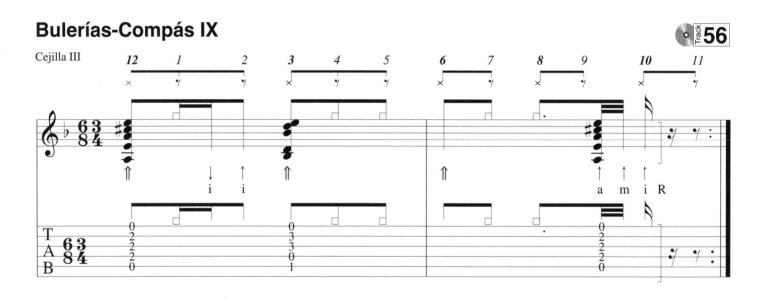

Bulerías-Compás X

Cejilla III

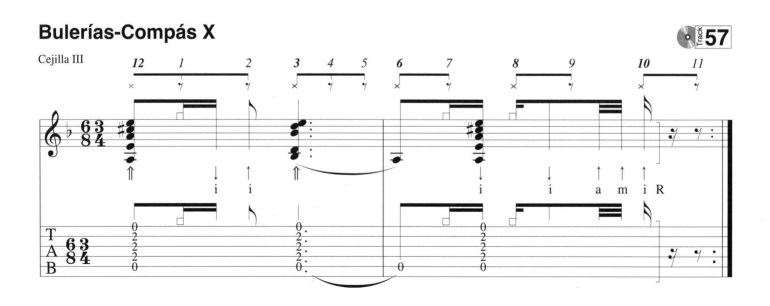

Here is yet another kind of **Bulerías** which were used by the older *tocaores* for the *acompañamiento*. The little finger of the left hand has to execute an *apagado* after each stroke. Don't spend too much time playing this exercise, because the little finger tires very quickly which is bad for the tendons.

You could play a chord change on the accented *3* after *Mi⁷* and change it back to *La* on the *rasgueo* before beat *10*. In this case, it would be a **Bulería** in La-major.

Bulerías-Compás XI

Cejilla III

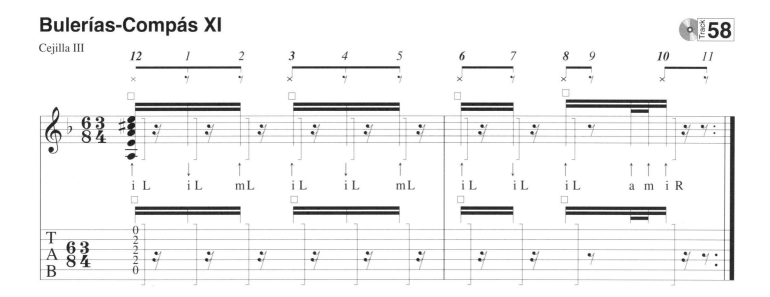

Bulerías-Compás XII is only a preliminary exercise to the following *compás* exercises. In the first version, *i* only strikes down and up except for the last eighth (quaver) and a stresses the accents with a *golpe*. In the second version, *p* only plays the accents together with the a-golpe and *i* only serves as accompaniment. This technique is called *La Horquilla*. *p* doesn't necessarily have to play a downstroke on all strings; it will suffice to strike ⑤, ④ and ③.

La Horquilla

Bulerías-Compás XII

Cejilla III

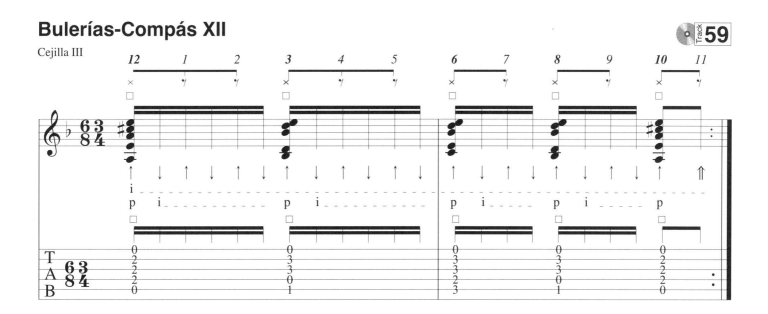

LESSON 8

Bulerías-Compás XIII is identical with the previous exercise, except that *i* plays no more downstrokes on the sixteenths (semiquavers) on beats *1, 2, 4, 5, 7* and *9*. If this causes rhythmic problems, you can pretend to execute the downstrokes at first, i.e. *i* plays a downstroke, but without touching the strings. To play the next upstroke, *i* must go down again, anyway. On the upstrokes, *i* only has to touch the treble strings.

The second version of the stroke is rather special. There is no reason for it, but it sounds nice if you can play it easily. The third version is *horquilla* again.

In the following exercises, you should stick to the fingerings of the right hand. It is hard to notice a difference at first glance, but if you practise long enough and compare the individual *compáses* with each other, you will probably hear the nuances.

Bulerías-Compás XIII

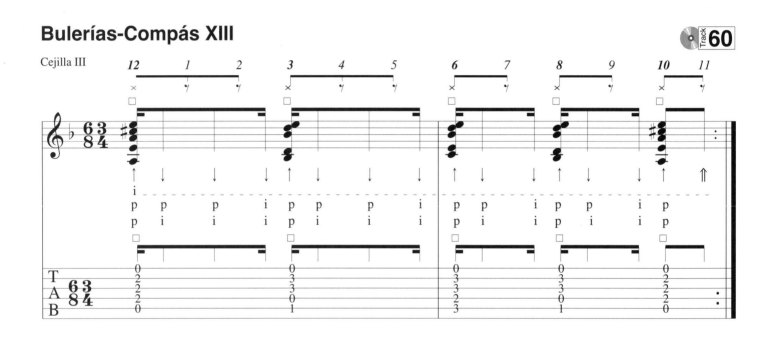

Bulerías-Compás XIV

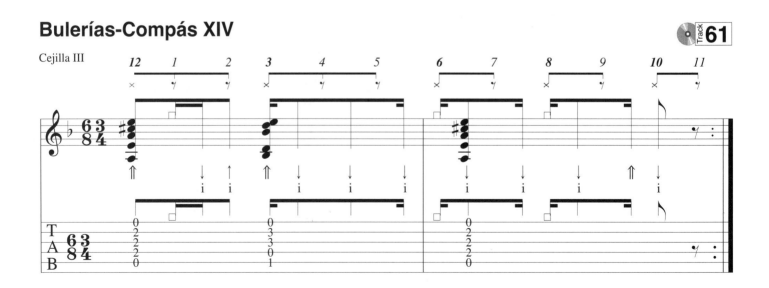

Bulerías-Compás XV

Cejilla III

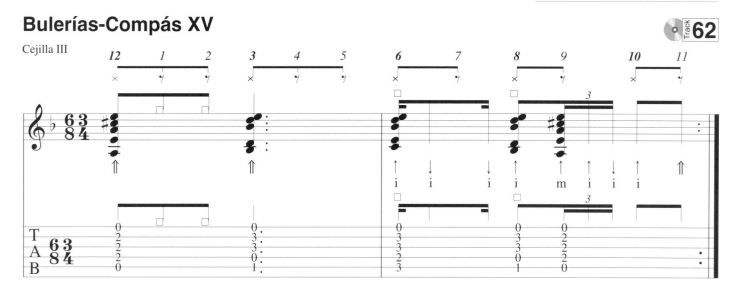

Bulerías-Compás XVI

Cejilla III

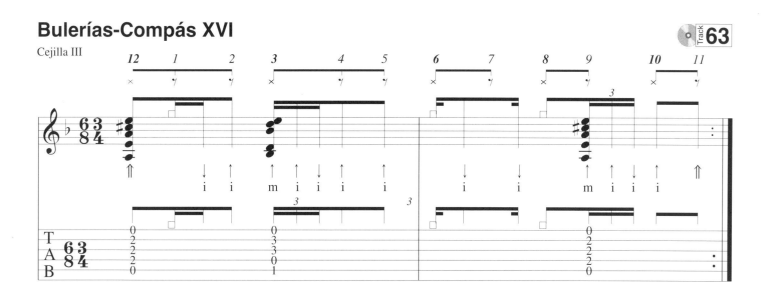

Bulerías-Compás XVII

Cejilla III

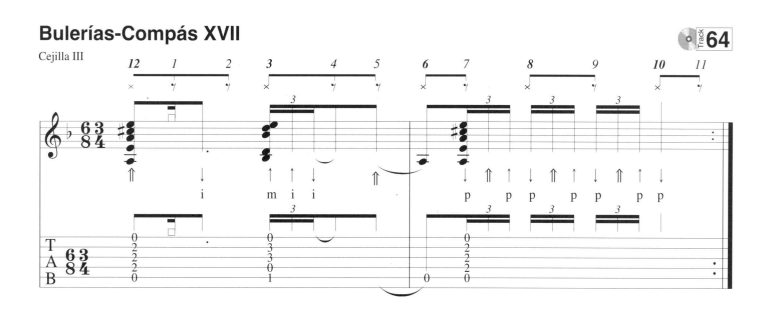

LESSON 8

Bulerías-Compás XVIII
Cejilla III

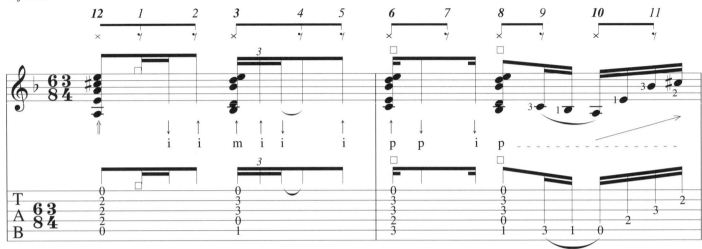

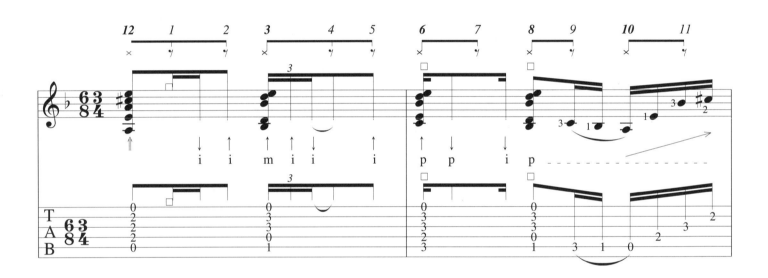

pregunta – respuesta – desarrollo

These examples of *compáses* could be continued ad infinitum. However, it is less motivating to practise the compáses individually – although every good *tocaor* has a great number of these *compás* variations in his repertoire.

The previous 18 *compáses* can now be joined together in any order whatsoever or, more precisely, you can improvise with them. The knack is in joining them well and playing them with the correct *aire*. That is why I again recommend listening to as many guitarists as possible. You will definitely come across some of these *compáses* if, of all things, you don't listen to recordings from the first half of the 20th century.

It is far more interesting and varied to mix these *compáses* with *falsetas*, although there are many *tocaores* who can captivate and fascinate their audience only with their *ritmo*. Here are three examples which can be perfectly joined together.

Columpio I (Bulerías) starts with the line *Intro;* lines 2 and 3 serve to "get into the groove." They could also be called the guitarist's *temple*, even though this expression doesn't exist in the *toque*. Lines 4 to 6 are the *ritmo*, ending with a *cierre*.

Columpio I (Bulerías)

Cejilla III

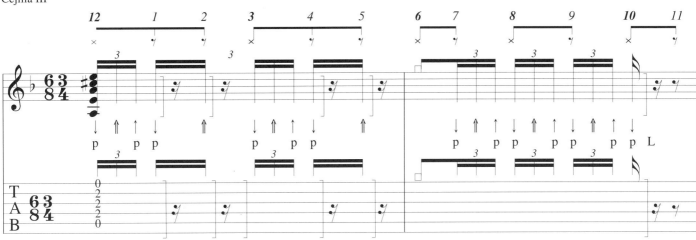
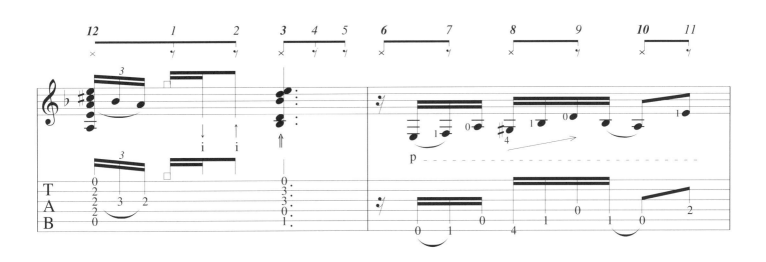
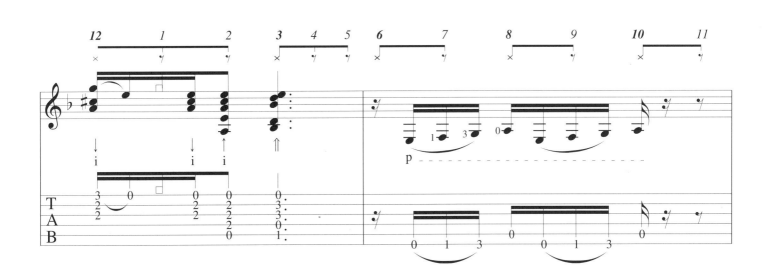

LESSON 8

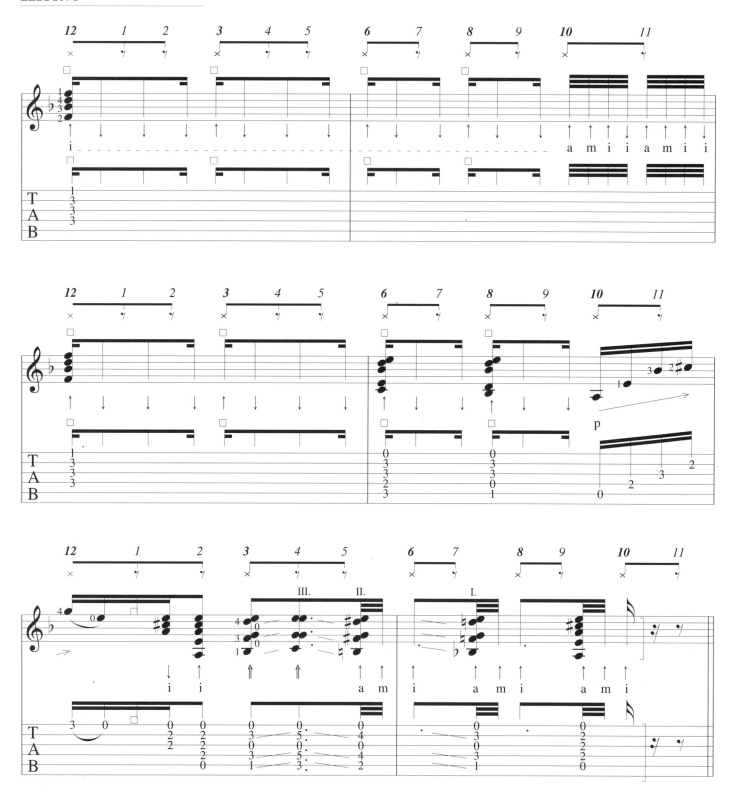

Columpio II (Bulerías) is rather easy in order to demonstrate the form of a classical *falseta*. Bars 3 and 4 are the *pregunta* (question), bars 5 and 6 are the *respuesta* (response) and bars 7 to 10 are the *desarrollo* (development). The *desarrollo* should always be as long as the *pregunta* and the *respuesta* combined. Unfortunately, many *tocaores* no longer stick to this rule.

The rhythmic sequence is also interesting. Whereas the *pregunta* and *respuesta* are played in alternating ⁶/₈ and ³/₄ time, the *desarrollo* is played in ³/₄ time (see foot rhythm indicated above the line).

Columpio II (Bulerías)

Cejilla III

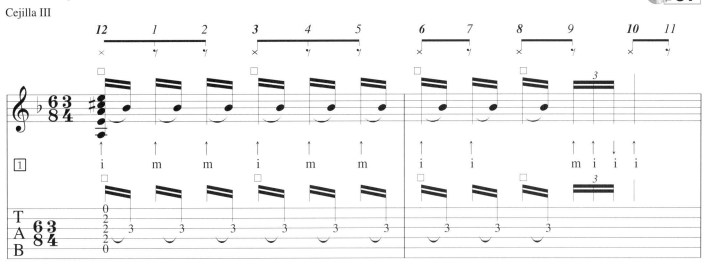
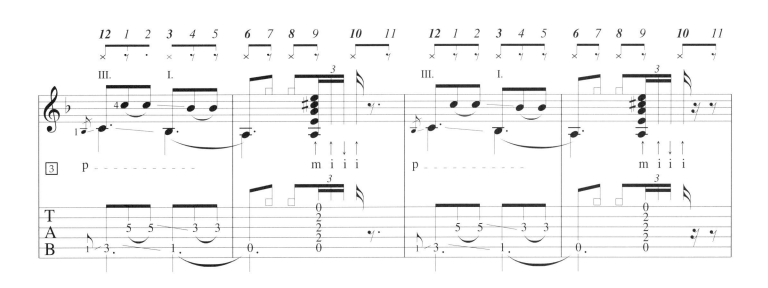
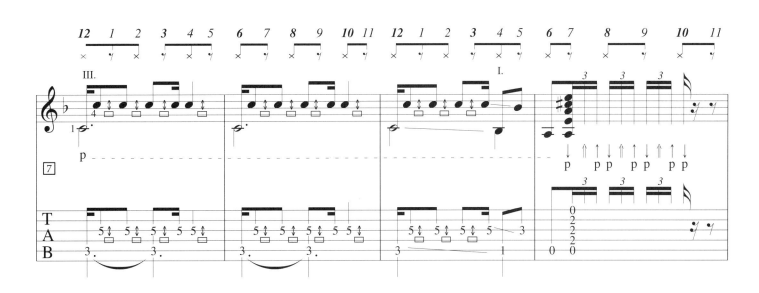

LESSON 8

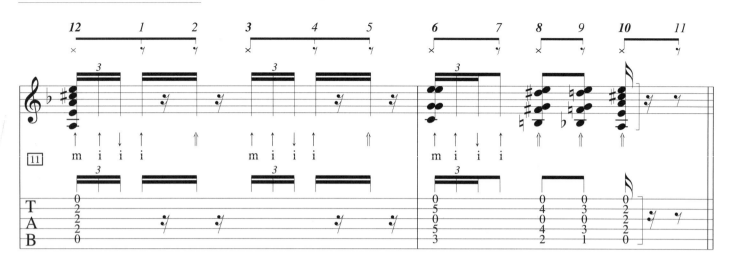

Columpio III (Bulerías)

Cejilla III

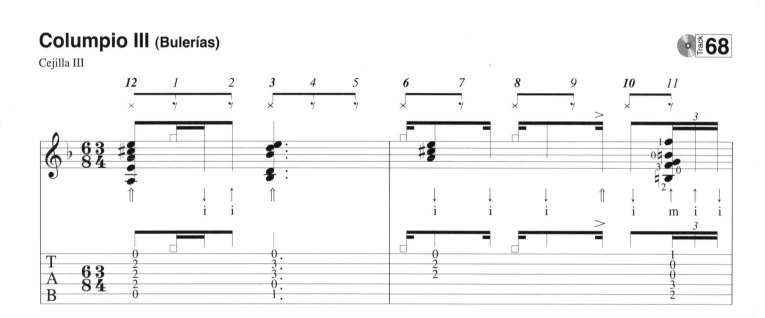

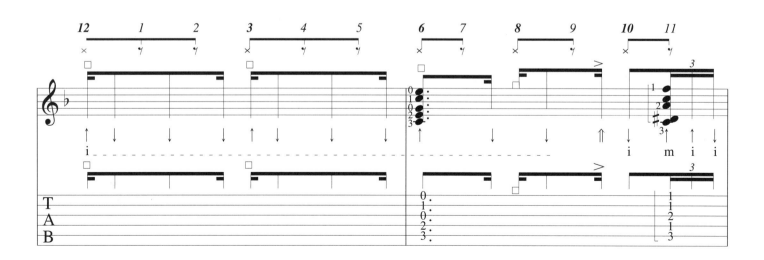

Bulerías I

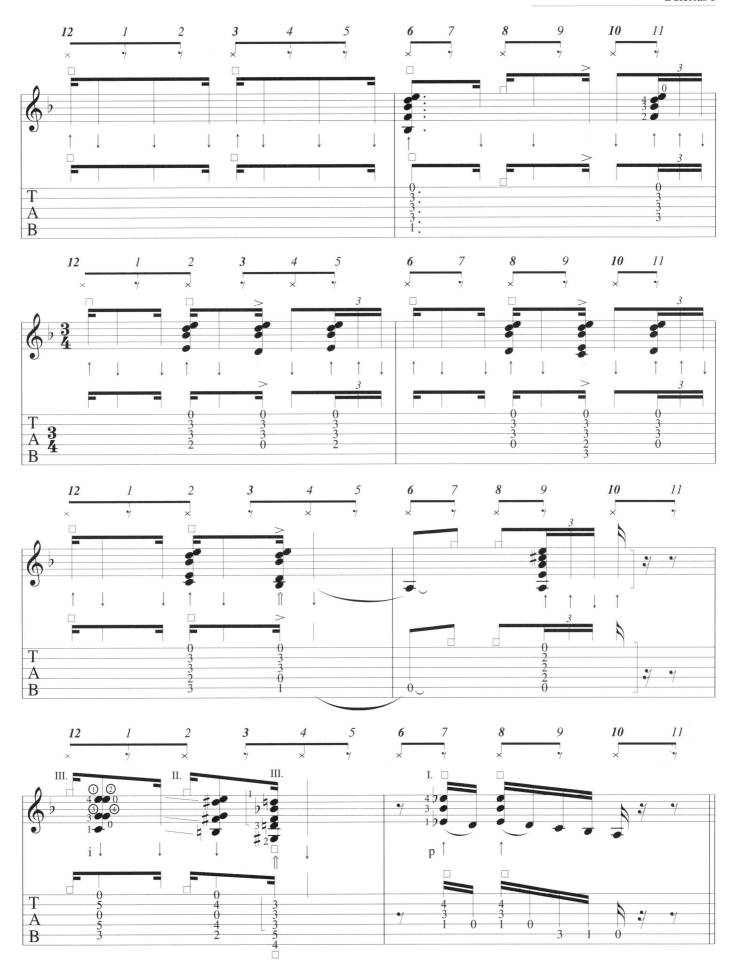

Antonio Amador

Primo mio

LESSON 9

Alzapúa

**Alzapúa I - III
(Exercises)**

**Alzapúa IV - VI
(Bulerías)**

Camarón (1950 - 1992) Photo: Dr. Walter Hilber

Alzapúa

The *alzapúa* is probably one of the most interesting Flamenco guitar techniques. Since it doesn't exist in any other kind of guitar music, colleagues from other genres often ask me how it works. And since it is mostly played very fast, it is absolutely impossible to see the sequence of strokes.

"Púa" is the plectrum and "alzar" means "to lift" or "to raise." Since the *alzapúa* is only played with the thumb, this means that *p* plays downstrokes and upstrokes across one or more strings.

More often than not, the *alzapúa* is played across three strings. The best way of describing the sequence of strokes is as a threefold movement, which doesn't mean, however, that it has to be a triad.

Movement 1: *p* begins with a downstroke on the middle string of the group of three strings (see picture 9.1), in this case ⑤. To emphasise this downstroke you can execute an additional *golpe* with *a*.

Movement 2: The downstroke is followed by an upstroke with the back of the nail (see picture 9.2).

Movement 3: and here is the trick and the most important part of the whole technique. *p* now plays the lowest string of the group of three, in this case ⑥, *apoyando* (see picture 9.3) and returns to its basic position on the middle string of the group of three (⑤) to start the whole thing from the beginning. It is important not to lift *p* from the string before repeating the threefold movement, but to execute the downstroke with *p* from its new position, in this case ⑤.

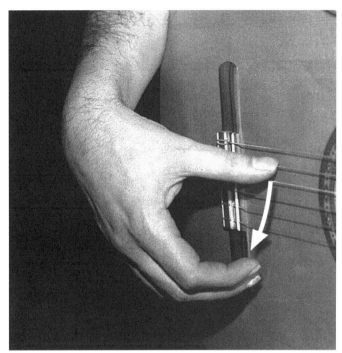

Picture 9.1 — Downstroke

Picture 9.2 — Upstroke

Picture 9.3 — Apoyando on a single string

LESSON 9

As long as no *golpe* is executed in addition to the *alzapúa*, *i*, *m* and *a* should be placed on ① so that the hand remains steady. The only source of movement is the large joint of the thumb. Later, once you can play this technique smoothly and fluently, you can strike with more force by turning the forearm and anchoring the thumb.

Alzapúa I:

Actually, this exercise is no typical *alzapúa*, but it is very suitable because the group of three, ④ ⑤ ⑥, is not changed. Since the thumb makes quite a large movement at first, it's not the end of the world if ③ sometimes resonates as well. And this is the sequence of strokes: *p* is placed on ⑤ and then plays a downstroke ↑ across ⑤ and ④. This is followed by an upstroke ↓ across the same pair of strings. Now the single string ⑥ is played *apoyando* ↗ (i.e. with a rest stroke). After that, *p* rests on ⑤ and is not lifted before playing ⑤ and ④ again.

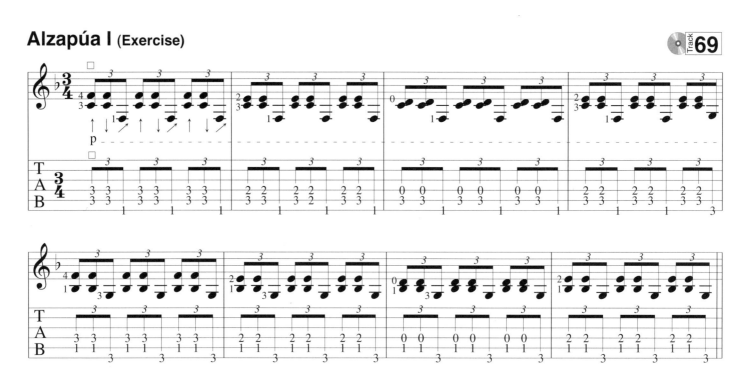

Alzapúa II:

Make sure that the melody, i.e. the single note, changes strings, and therefore also the group of three. Fingers 3 and 4 rest on b♭-③ and d-② throughout.

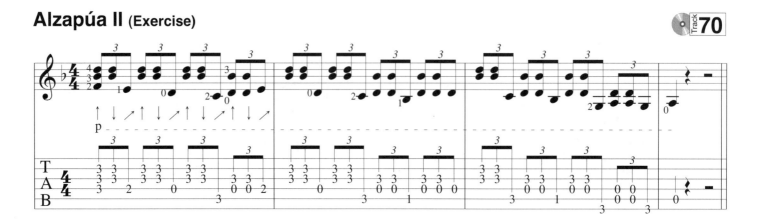

Alzapúa III:
This exercise is basically identical with the previous one, except that you begin on the single note which is played *apoyando*. If you can play both exercises quite smoothly, you should practise with a metronome and put an accent on the first eighth (quaver) of each triad. The different *aires* of these exercises will then be clearly audible.

Alzapúa III (Exercise)

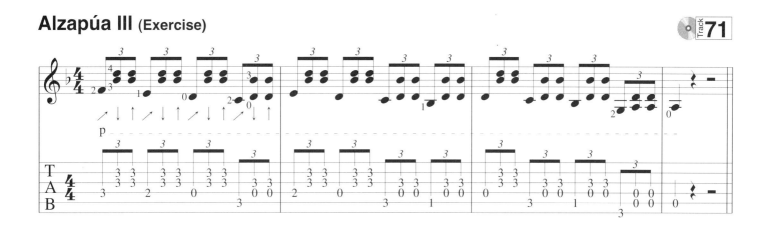

Bulerías-Compás IV: is written in the *compás* of the **Bulerías** and can be used as an *intro*. The *alzapúa* is notated in 6/8 time, the *ritmo*, or rhythmic filling, in 3/4 time. The *alzapúa* in bars 1 - 3 and 10 - 13 is a bit more difficult to read, because the A is either played on ⑥ or on ⑤. In this case, the tablature is clearer.

Bars 1 - 3 are identical: downstroke with *p,* upstroke with *p* across ⑤ ④, followed by a single note *(apoyando)* on ⑥. The last two eighths (quavers) are of course also played *apoyando*. The index finger of the left hand remains at the second position on e-④. If *p* still strikes ③ accidentally sometimes, the index finger should play the a-③ as a half-barre.

The *tresillos* in bars 4, 5, 9 and 13 are only played on ⑥ ⑤ ④ ③ . From bar 6 up to the penultimate eighth (quaver) in bar 9, the little finger and the ring finger rest on d-⑤ and g-④. The golpe on the first sixteenth (semiquaver) in bars 6 to 12 can be left out at the beginning. *i, m* and *a* always rest on ① if no *golpe* is executed.

Since the fingers must be overextended in this exercise, you can start out by placing the *cejilla* at the third fret. There's no point in looking for a different fingering: this is the best one.

Alzapúa IV (Bulerías)

Cejilla III

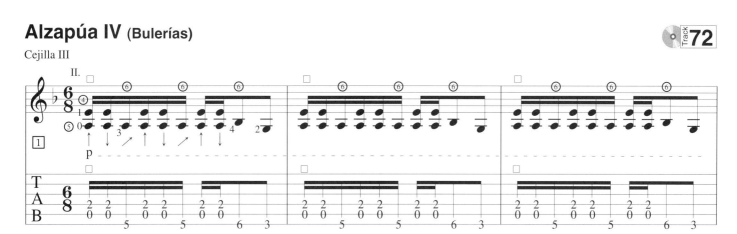

LESSON 9

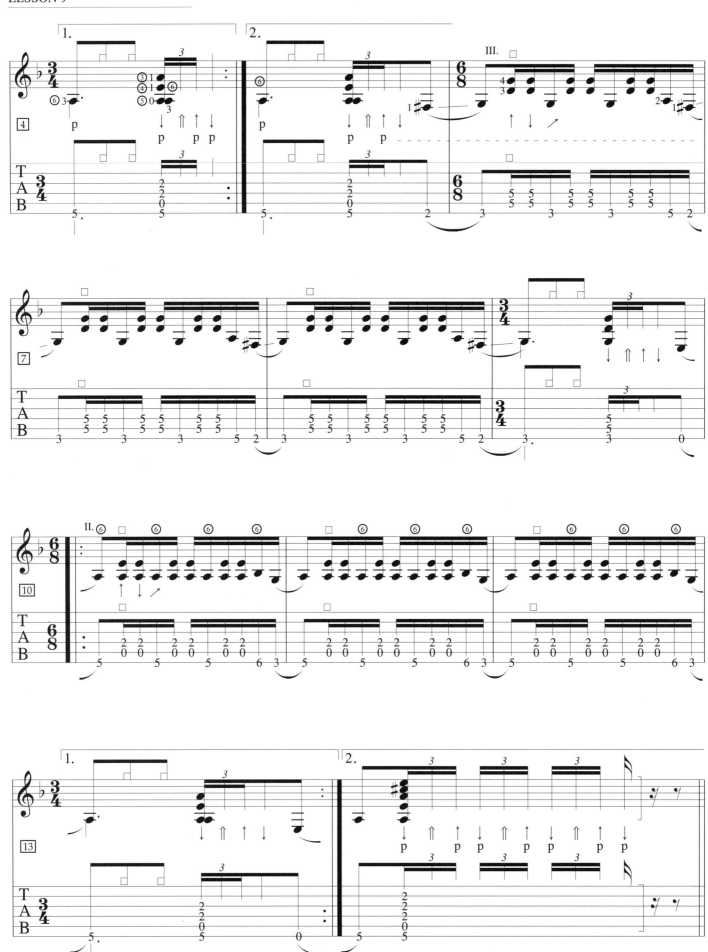

60

Here is an *alzapúa* played across two strings. LUIS YANCE, MANUEL DE HUELVA and NIÑO RICARDO used to play this old *falseta*. Nobody knows who created it.

Alzapúa VI is the modern version.

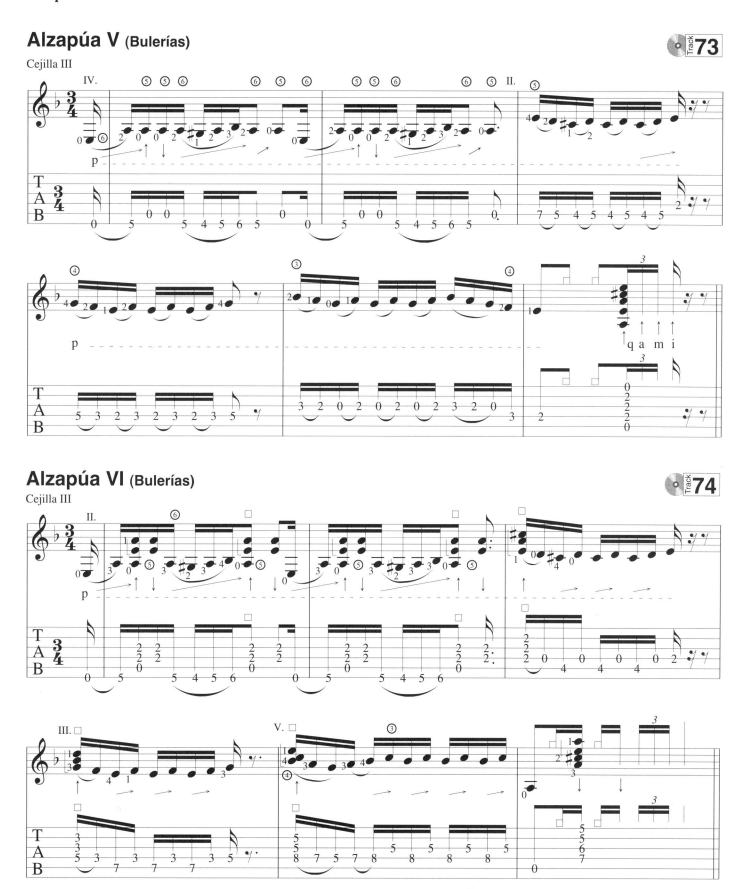

El Taranto

Lela De Fuenteprado

Photos: Claudia Ammann

LESSON 10

Soleá
Mantón VIII - XI

Alegrías en Mi I - V

Caí II - V
(Alegrías en Do)

Bulerías II
Columpio IV - V

Quejío IV (Tarantos)

Naino VI - VIII
(Tangos)

La Alhambra: Patio de los Arrayanes

Photo: Graf-Martinez

Soleá

Now that I have explained all Flamenco guitar techniques, this chapter is about *falsetas* and *compáses* of selected *estilos*. As I mentioned in the preface, *falsetas* or *compáses* should be learned by heart to be able to combine them freely – as is actually done in the *toque*.

Have a close look at bars 8 and 9 of **Mantón VIII** (Soleá). In bar 8, *p* actually plays across all strings up to ① and then plays alternating upstrokes and downstrokes with ⇑ on $Mi^{7/9}$ until the *tresillo* in bar 9.

In **Mantón IX** (Soleá), everything should be clear.

Mantón VIII (Soleá)

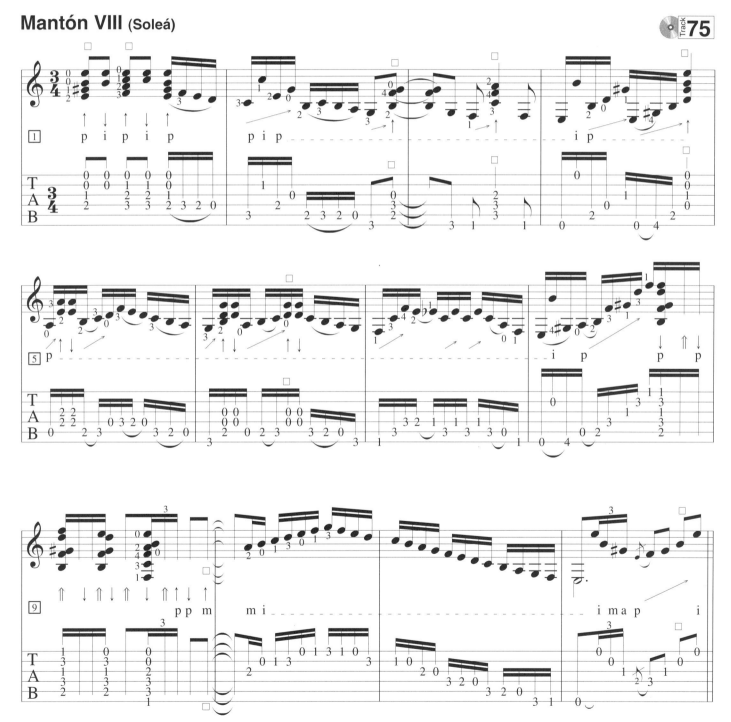

LESSON 10

Mantón IX (Soleá)

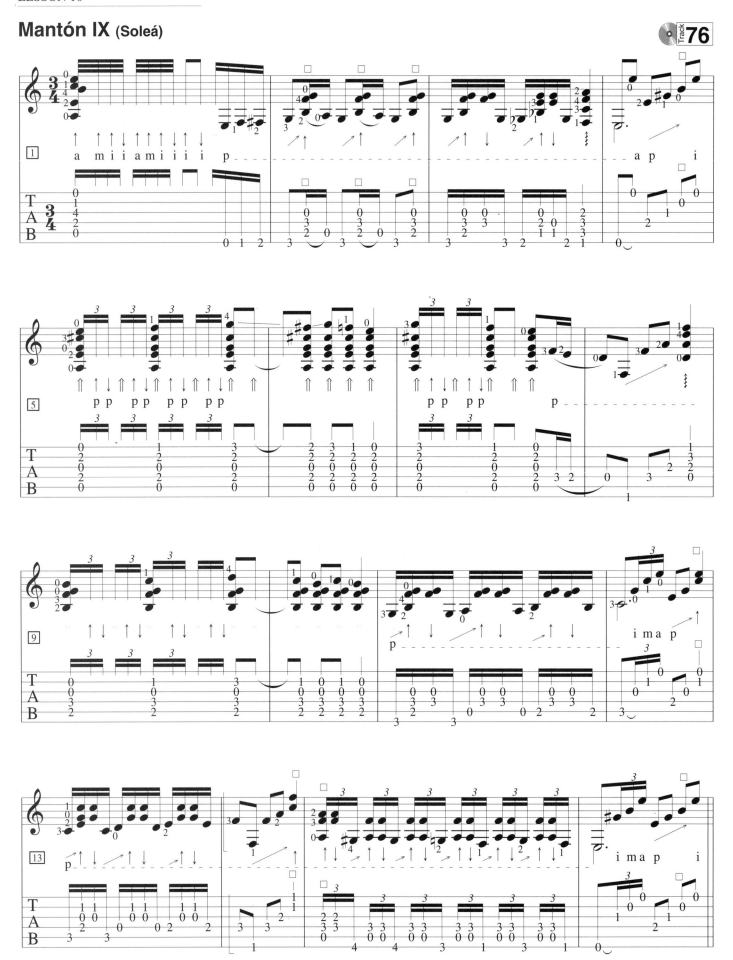

In this chapter about *soleá* I'd like to do without *compáses* – in this case playing chords – because a lot of them are included in the previous *soleás*. These *compáses* may be inserted between the *falsetas* notated here. Important: always keep to the *12-beat compás*.

To move from the ties in bar 1 to g♯③, the index finger needs to slide from the second to the first fret. In bars 6 and 8, the barre should be fingered on the appoggiatura. Note the transition from sixteenths (semiquavers) to sixteenth triplets (semiquaver triplets) in bar 11.

Mantón X (Soleá)

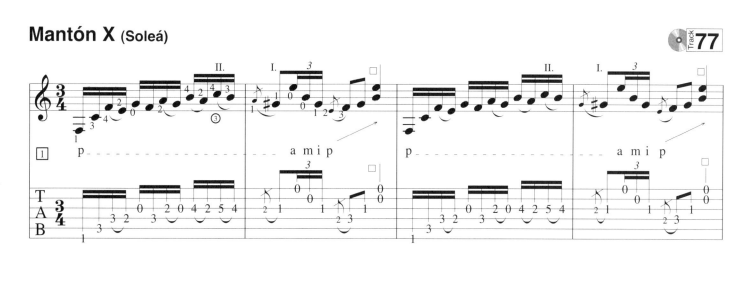

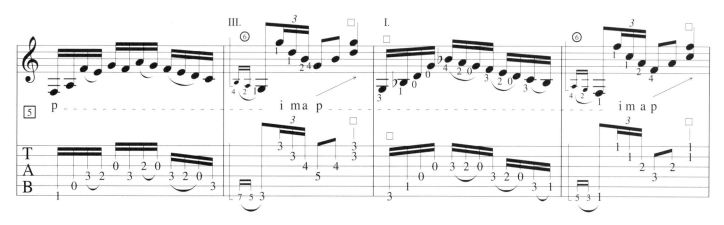

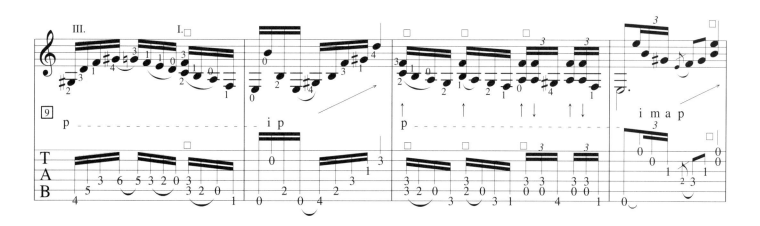

LESSON 10

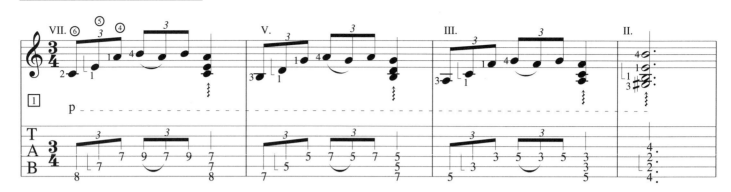

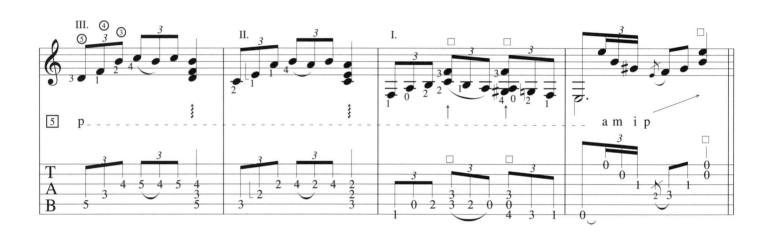

The *falseta* of **Mantón XI** (Soleá) is very suitable as an *introducción*. Do repeat the first line, because otherwise the *respuesta* will be missing. Bar 6 is the *Sol*-chord at the seventh position and bar 8 is the *Fa*-chord at the fifth position. Note the *ligados* in bars 9, 10 and 11. The *remate* in bar 12 is a *Mi*-chord at the fourth position. Don't play the upstrokes and downstrokes in bars 13 and 14 with too much emphasis; they only function as an accompaniment.

Mantón XI (Soleá)

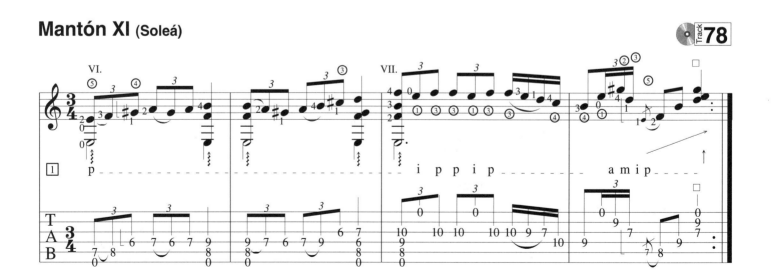

Soleá

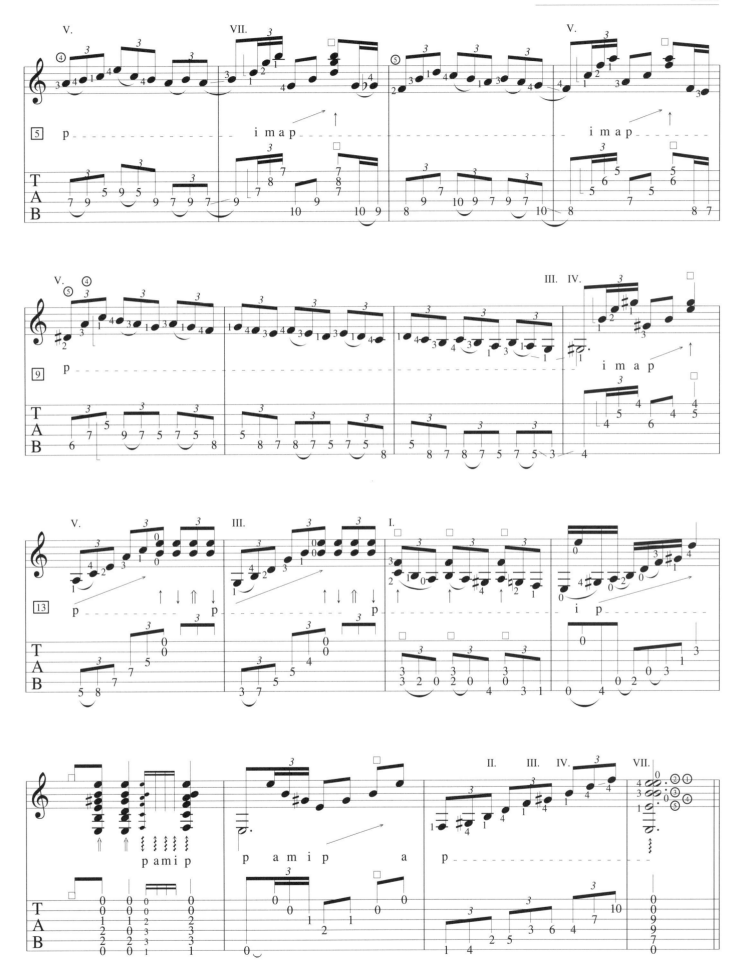

LESSON 10

Alegrías

The traditional *cante* accompaniment includes only two chords: the tonic and the dominant, or dominant seventh chord, respectively. You can play the *Alegrías* and all their derivatives in any key. The most common keys are *Mi*, *Do* and *La* major. The *Alegría* includes such a wide range of chord changes that it is impossible to set up a rule. Traditionally, the chord changes on 10. However, it is also possible to change the chord on the anticipated 9.

The following chord progression can be used as an *intro*.

Alegría en Mi I (Compás Exercise) — Track 79

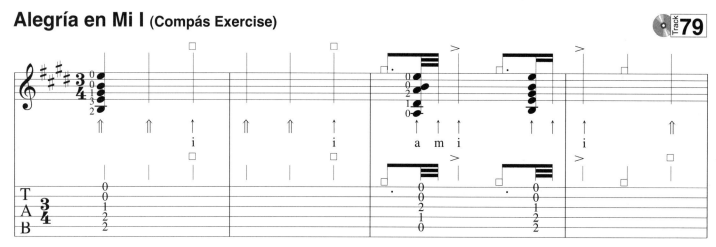

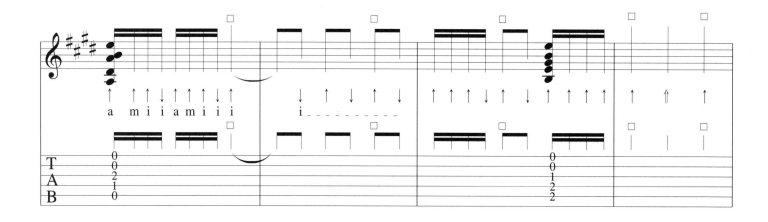

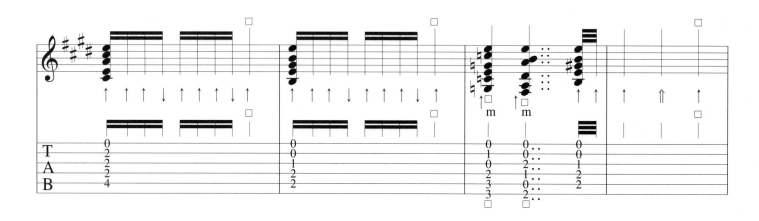

Alegrías

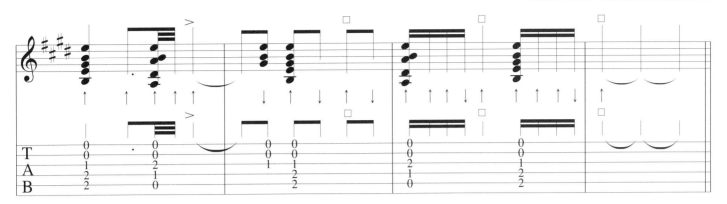

Each line of **Alegrías en Mi II** (Compás Exercises) can be used as a basic *compás* for the **Alegrías** – and they are only a few examples. The chord always changes on 3 and 10. The *remates,* beats 10 to 12, vary in this example, but this is not always the case. Here, too, the principle applies: the wider the range of the *tocaor's* repertoire, the more varied the *toque.*

Alegría en Mi II (Compás Exercise)

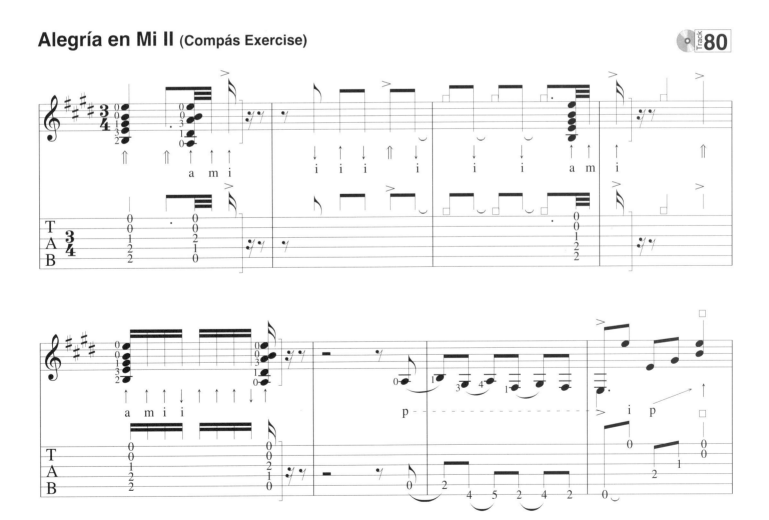

LESSON 10

Lela de Fuenteprado & Ensemble

Photo: Katrin Schandner

Alegría en Mi III (Intro)

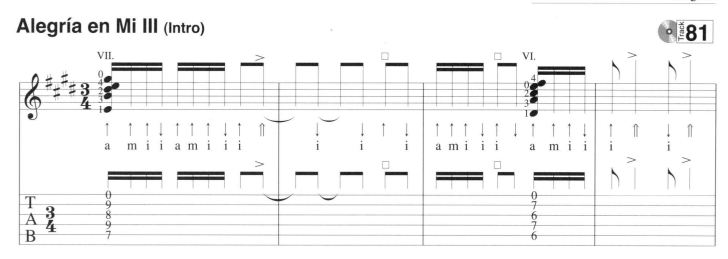
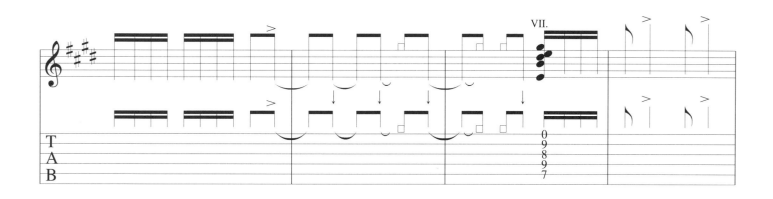
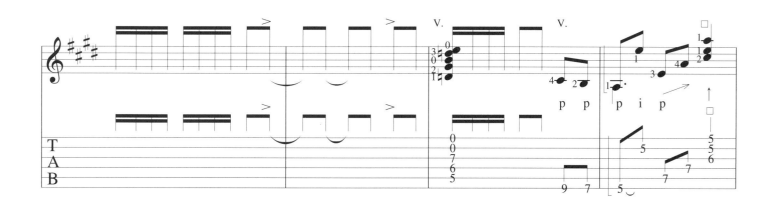
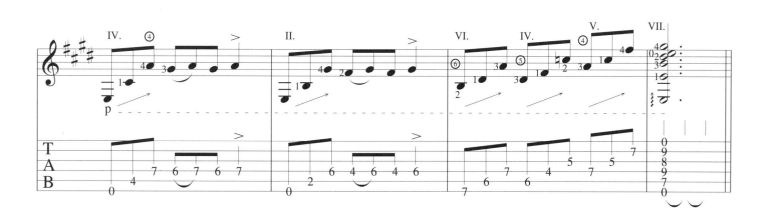

Alegría en Mi IV (Escobilla)

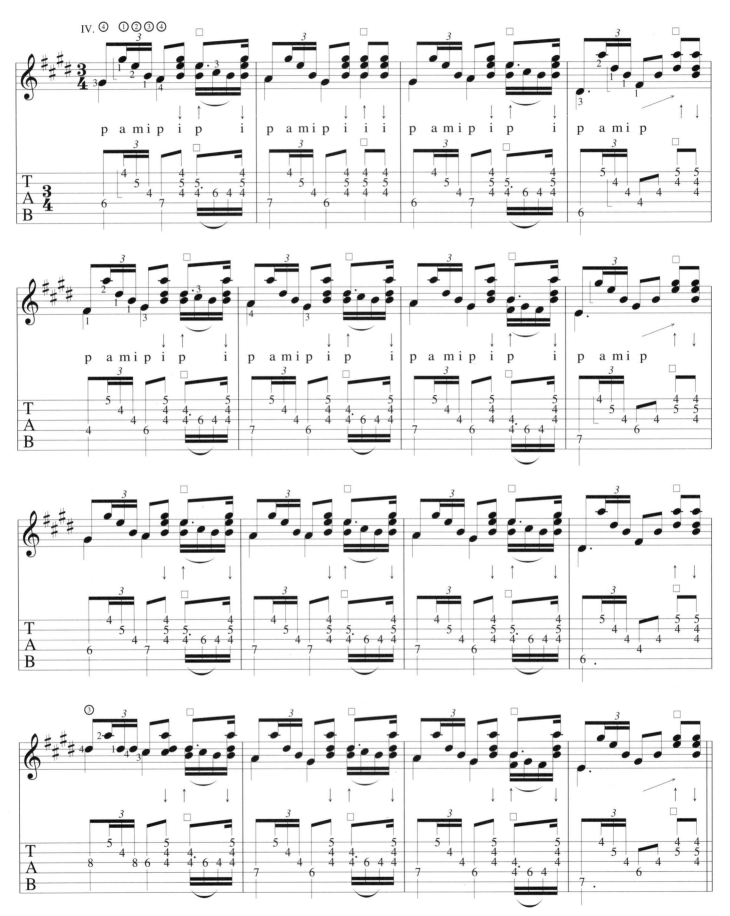

Alegría en Mi V (Puente)

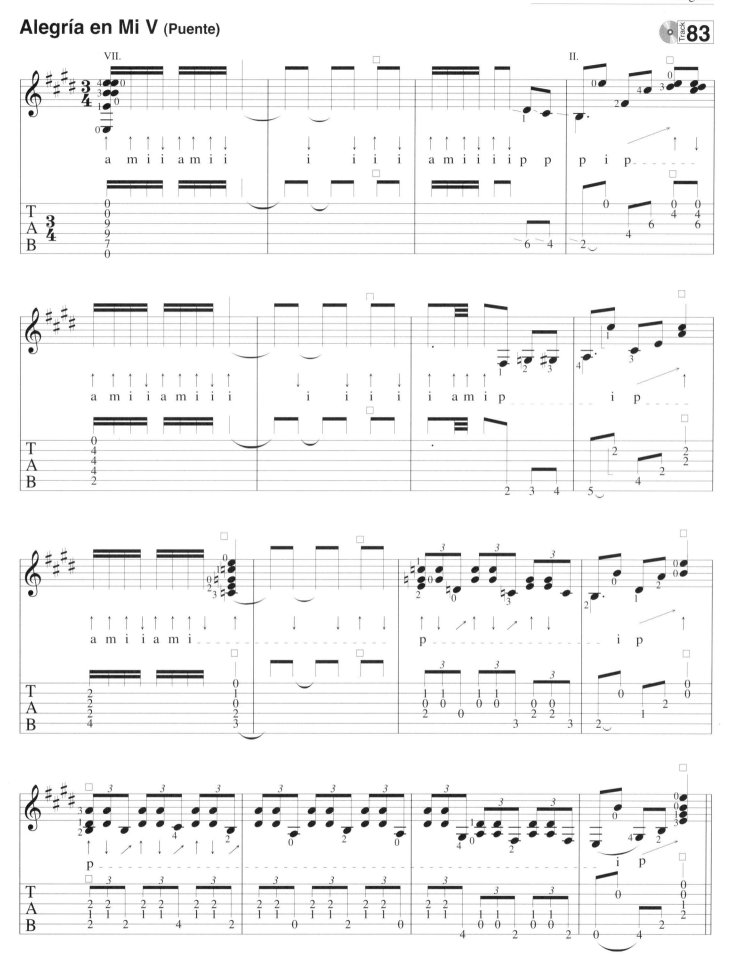

Caí II (Alegría en Do)

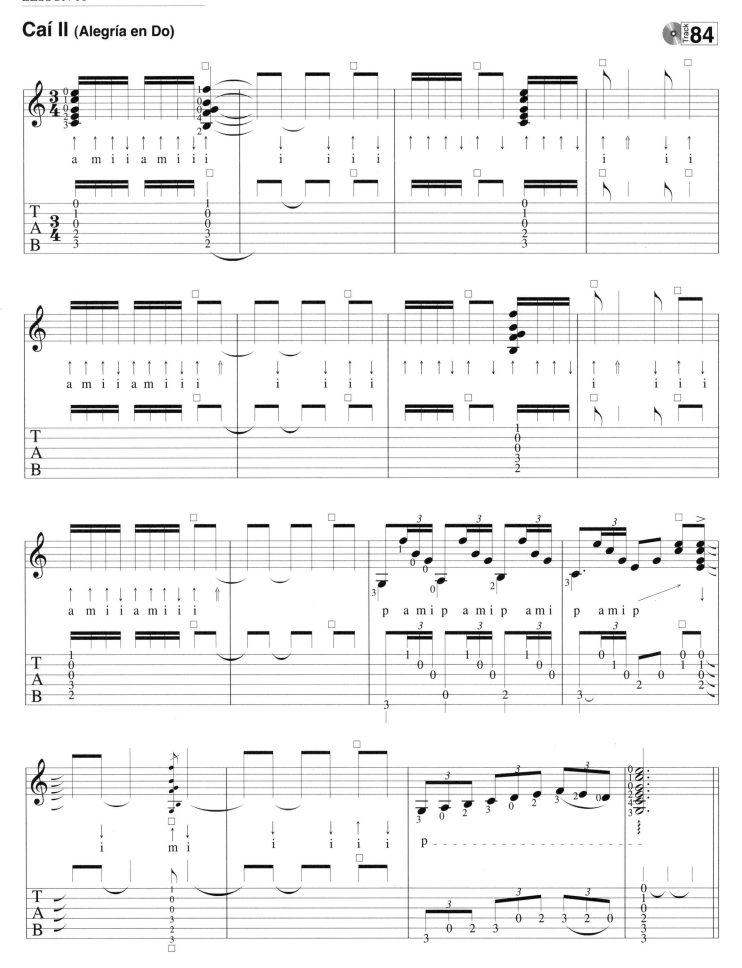

Alegrías

Caí III (Alegría en Do)

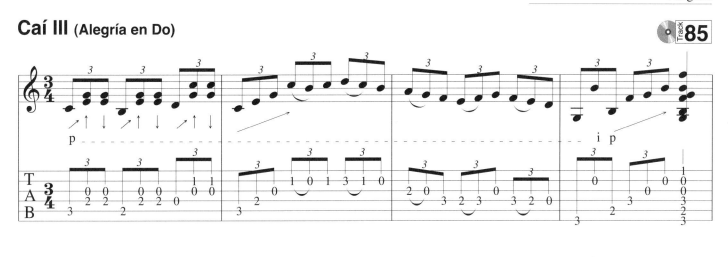
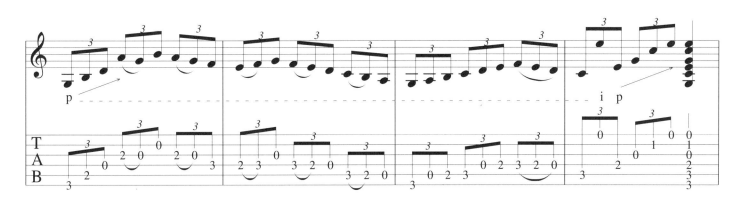
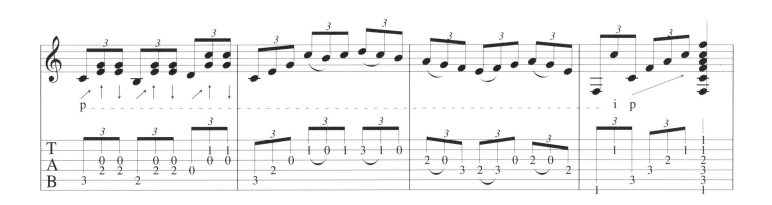
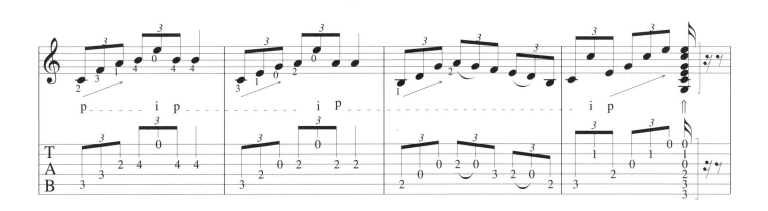

LESSON 10

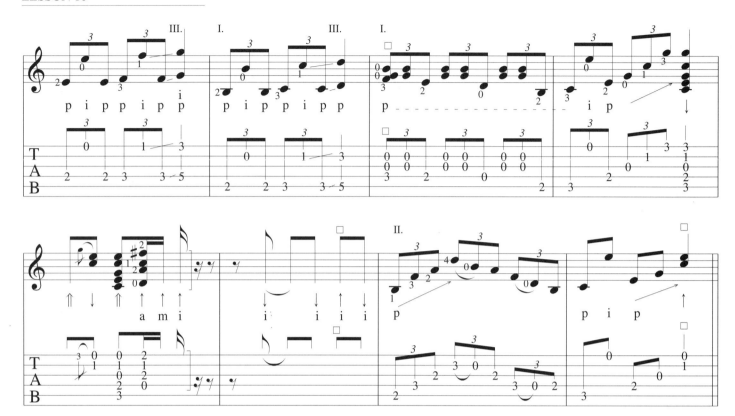

International Guitar workshop with Andrés Batista (1983 in Schorndorf)

Caí IV (Alegría en Do)

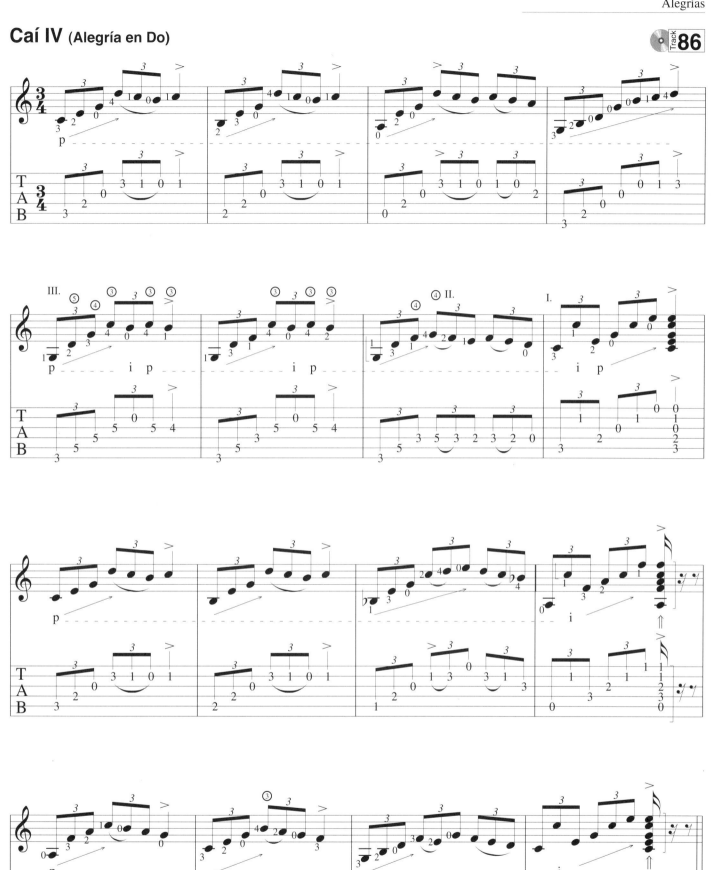

LESSON 10

Caí V (Alegría en Do)

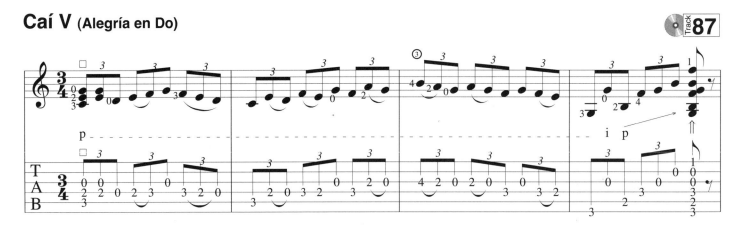
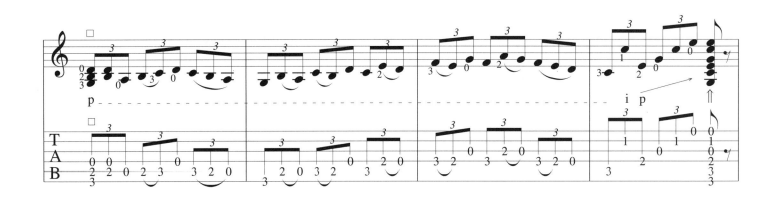
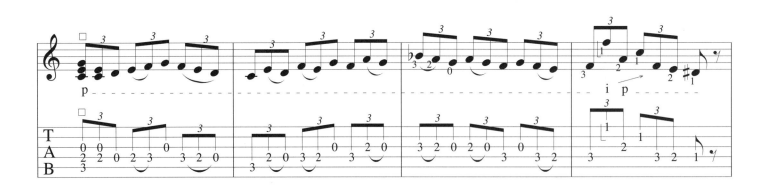
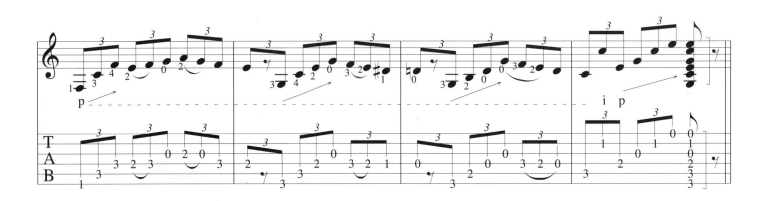

Bulerías II

Columpio IV (Bulerías Intro)

Cejilla III

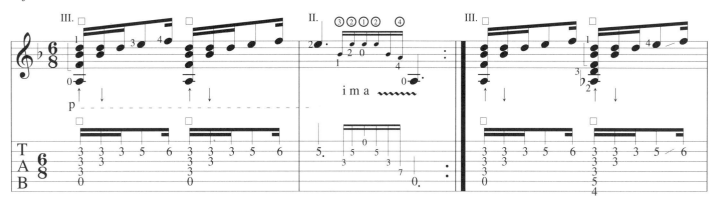
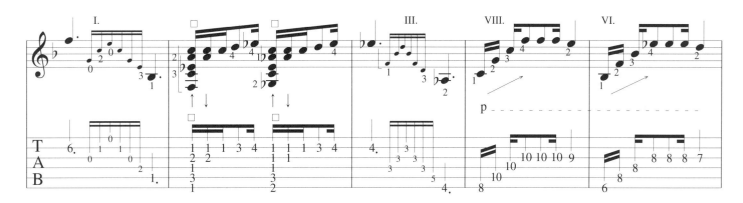
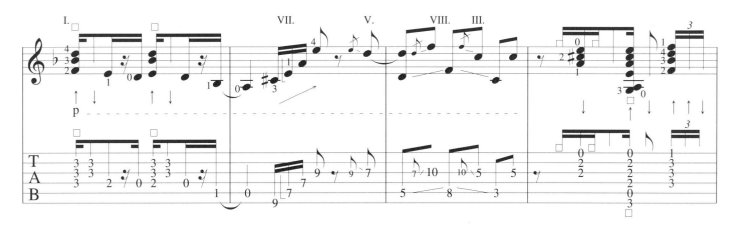
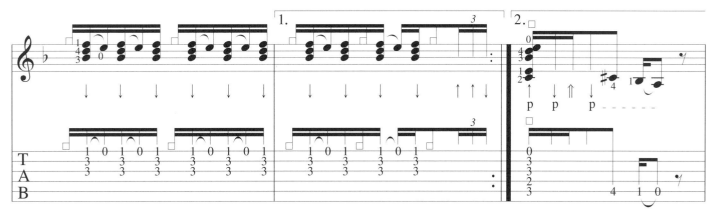

LESSON 10

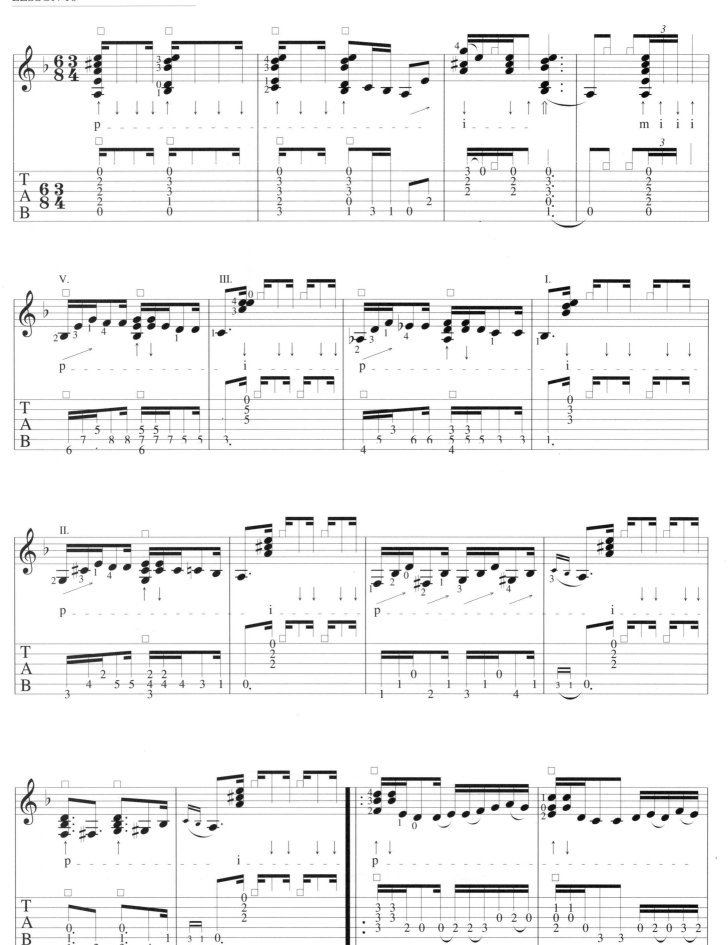

Bulerías II

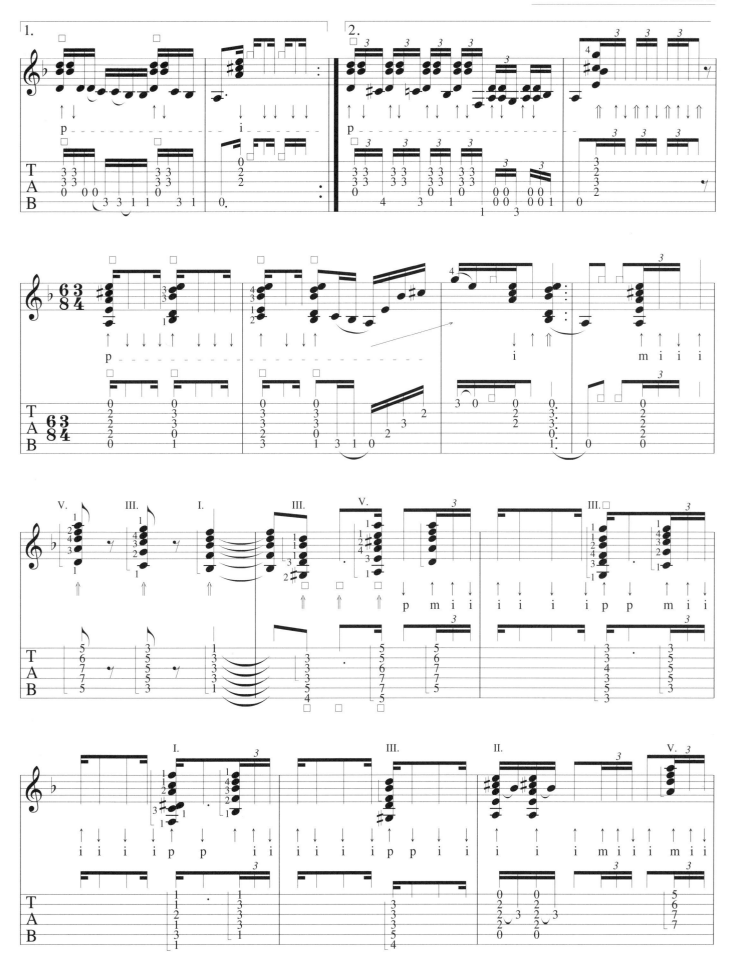

LESSON 10

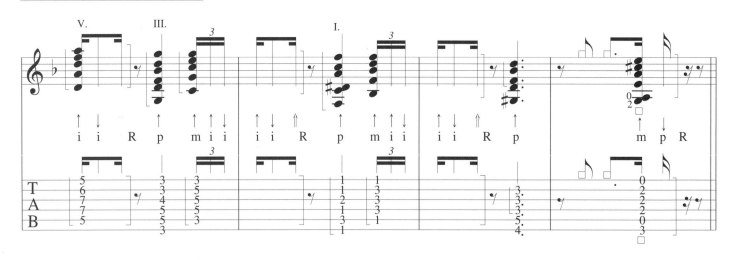

Andrés Batista and Gerhard Graf-Martinez (1982)

Columpio VI (Bulerías)

Cejilla III

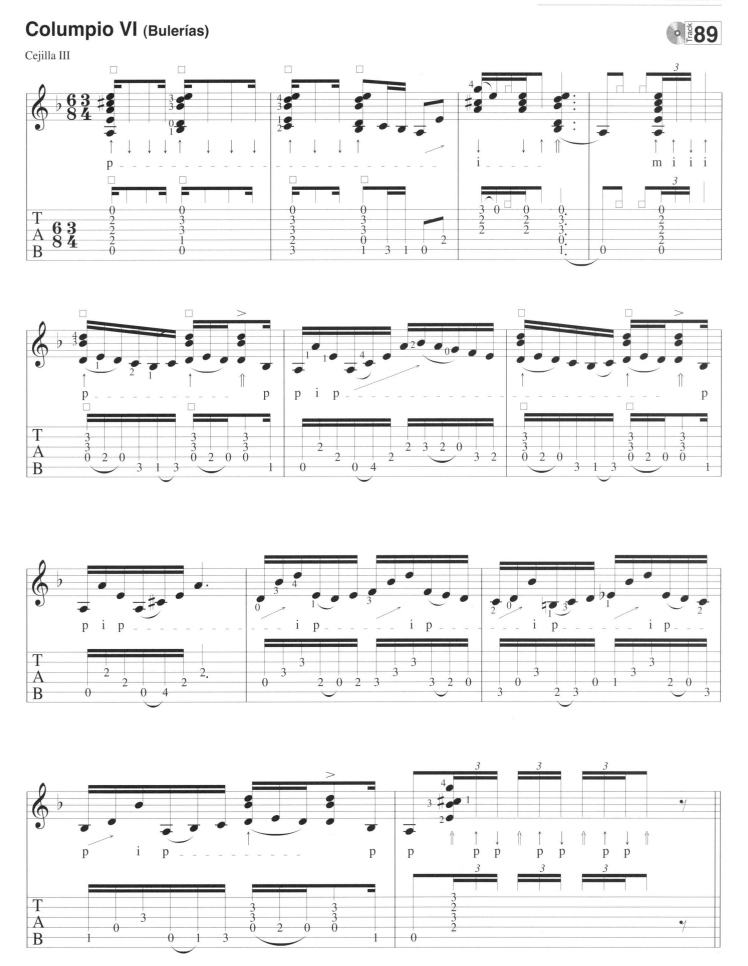

Quejío IV (Taranto)

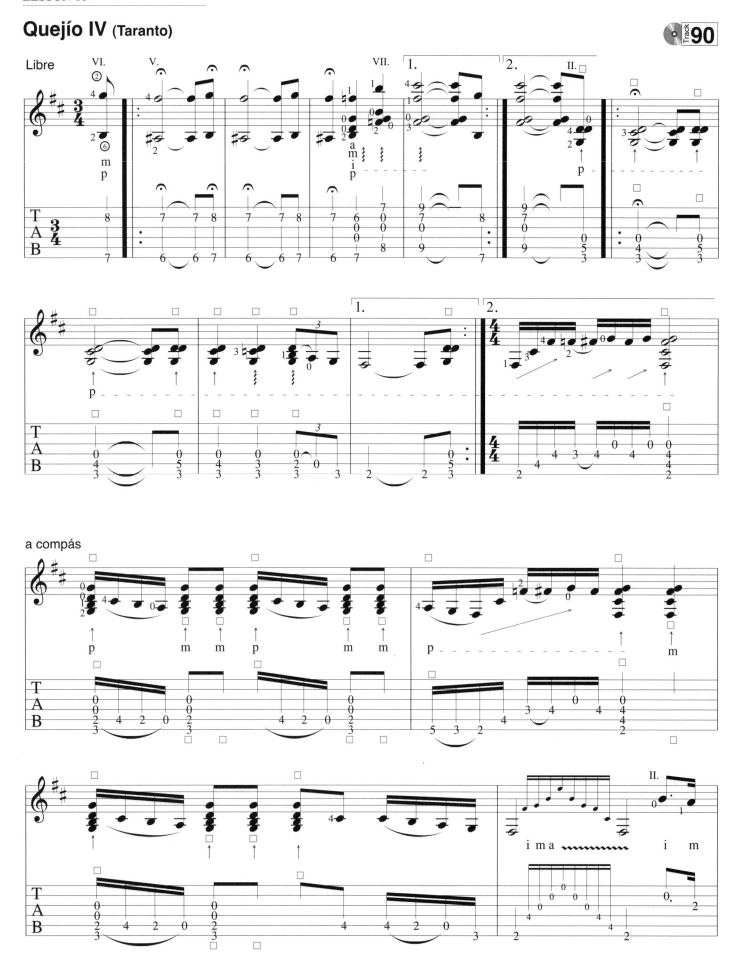

Tarantos

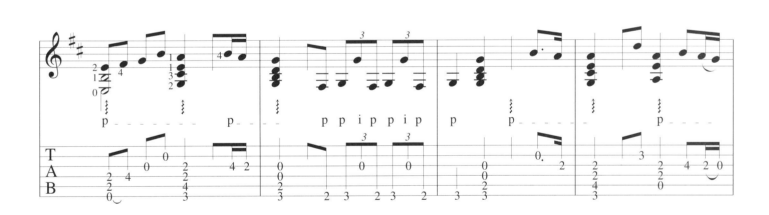
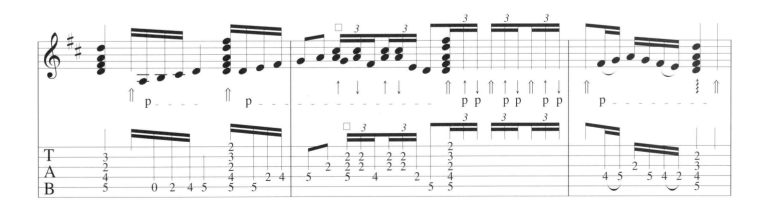

LESSON 10

88

Tangos

Naino VI (Tangos)

Cejilla III

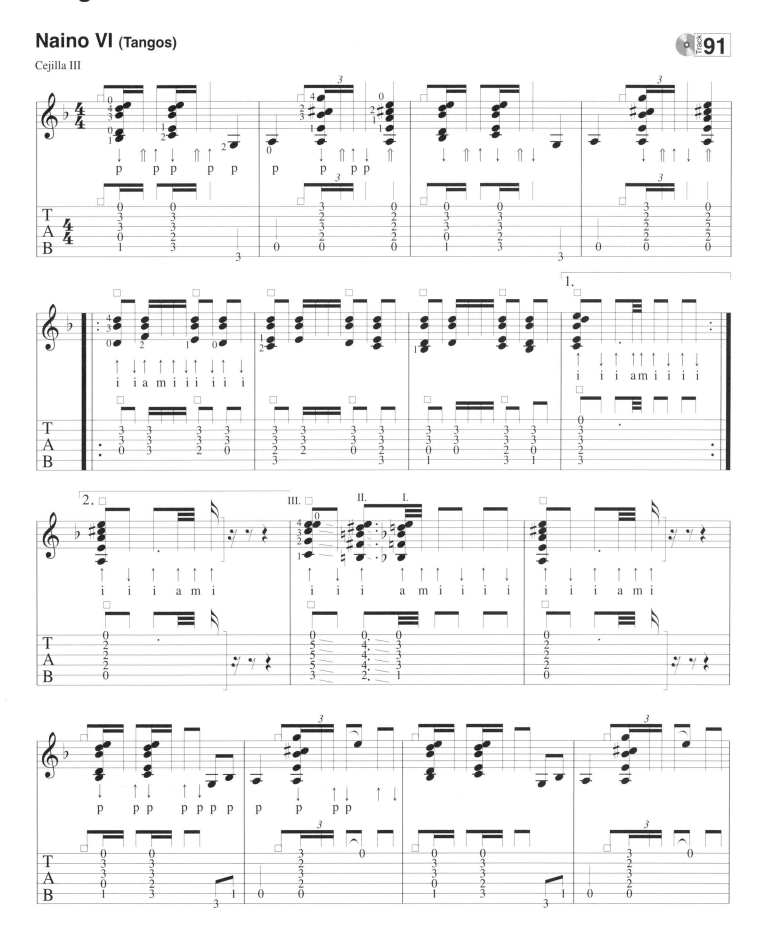

LESSON 10

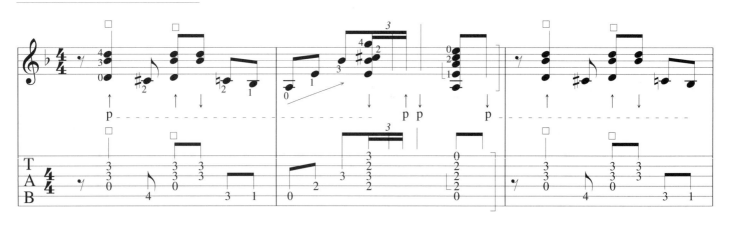
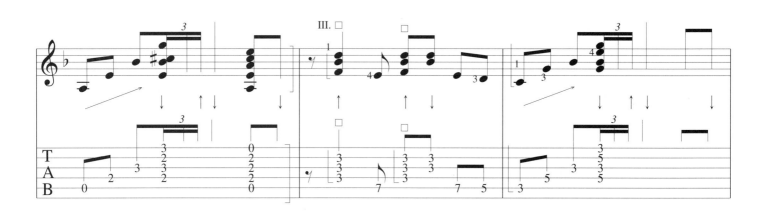
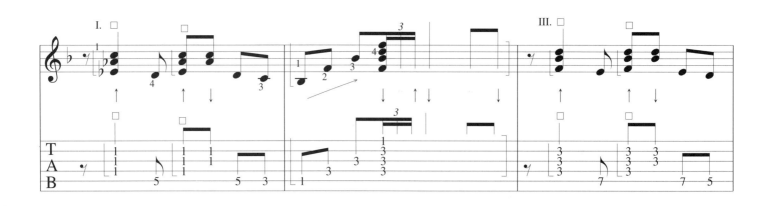
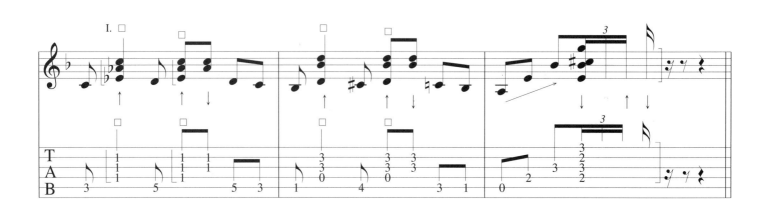

Naino VII (Tangos)

Cejilla III

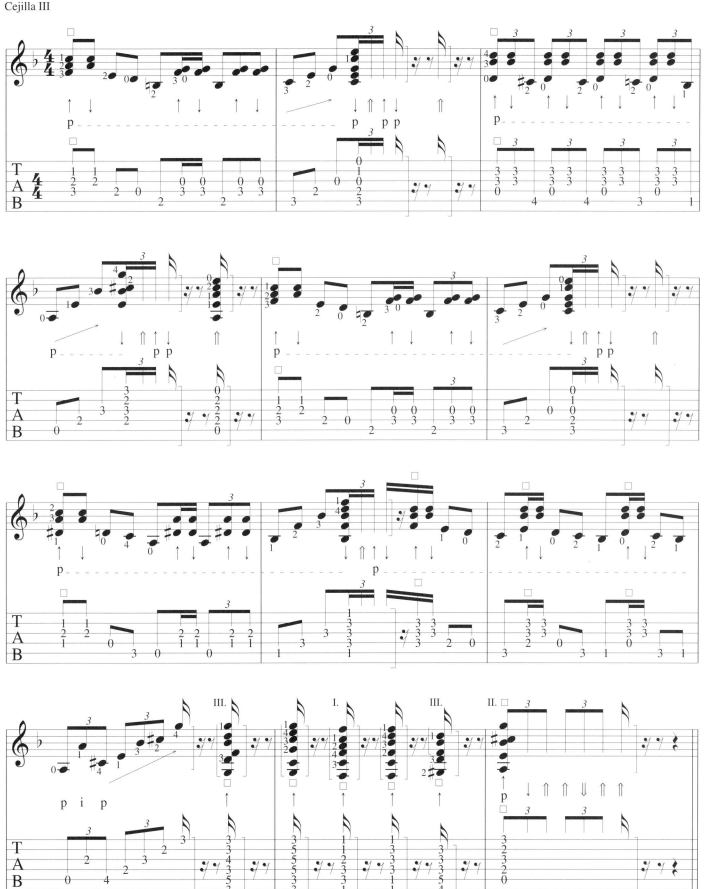

LESSON 10

Naino VIII (Tangos)

Cejilla III

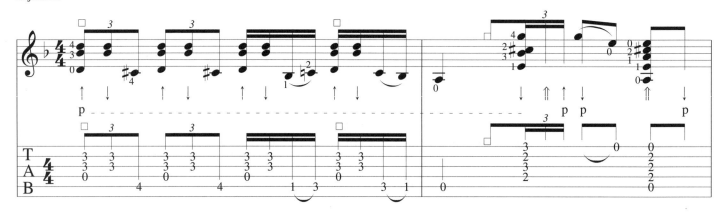
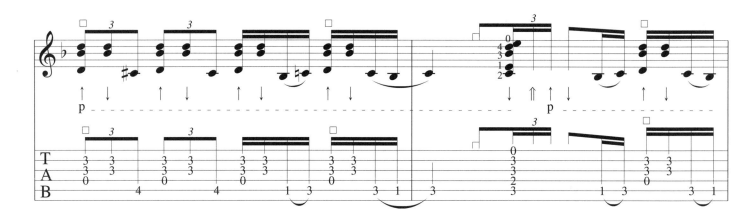
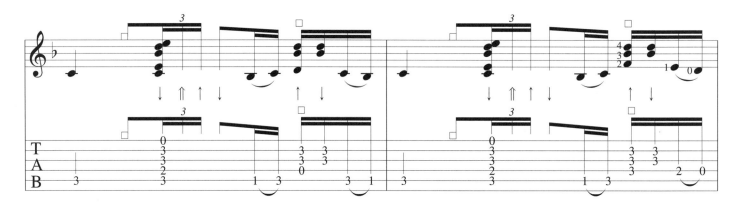
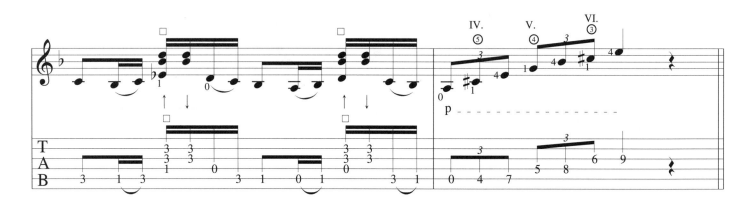

ESTILOS

Alborada ...

... Zorongo

Mariano de Delphina and Gerhard Graf-Martinez — Photo: Katrin Schandner

Estilos

Alborada *c, t;* folkloric serenade from Galicia and Valencia in the *compás* of the **Farruca.** The following example is the typical "falseta de Alborada" which is played accelerando at the end of the **Farruca** *de baile* before it changes into the finale.

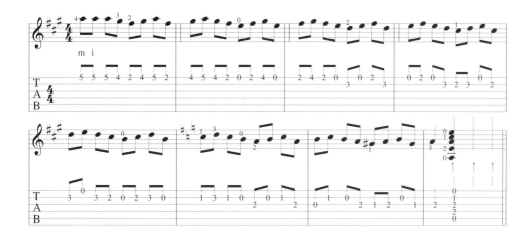

c = *cante (singing)*

b = *baile (dancing)*

t = *toque (guitar)*

Alboreás *c, t;* wedding chant of the *gitanos*. In the *compás* of the **Soleá por Bulerías.** The *gitanos* in Granada sing the **Alboreás** in the *compás* of the **Tangos.**

Alegrías *c, b, t;* cheerful *cante* and *baile*, influenced by the *Jota*. They probably originated in the "Guerra de Independencia" (war of independence) in Cadíz. Major/minor mode. The traditional cante needs no more than two chords: the tonic and the subdominant. As far as the structure is concerned, the **Alegrías** *de baile* is one of the most difficult forms. See **Volume I**, Lesson 2, and **Volume II**, Lesson 10.

Bambas *c;* of Hispanic origin. Similar to the **Nanas** and **Trillas**. A typical feature is the *columpio* rhythm. Played in major or minor; the end is often sung in the *modo dórico*.

Bamberas *c,b,t;* from the genre of the *cantes camperos*. The "flamencocized" form of the **Bambas** was created by the great *cantaora* NIÑA DE LOS PEINES. In the *compás* and *aire* of the **Soleá** in the *modo dórico*. There is a **Bamberas** by FOSFORITO which he sings in the *compás* of the **Fandango.**

Bandolás *c, t;* **Verdiales** with more Flamenco *aire* and slower. Probably influenced by the "Cante de Juan Breva." Possibly the successor of the "Cante de los **jabegotes**."

Bulerías *c, b, t;* the most flexible form of Flamenco. The word might have the following three origins: "burlería" (ridicule), "bulo" *(Romaní* for lie, untruth) or "bulicioso" (noisy).

ESTILOS

Major/minor as well as *modo dórico*. Derived from **Soleá** and **Jaleo.** The **Bulería** is often characterized by the use of melodies, sometimes entire *coplas* from different *estilos,* or folk songs, or the spontaneous invention of parts of the lyrics. The **Bulerías** are the prime example of the so-called *cante festeros:* songs sung at celebrations. Nowadays they are often performed with the deepness and seriousness of the *cante grande.* See Lesson 8, 9 and 10 in this volume.

Cabales *c, t;* a variation of the **Siguiriyas,** but sung in the major mode. It was created by EL FILLO and is often used as a *remate,* which is known as *macho* in the modern **Siguiriyas,** with a typical change to the major mode.

Caleseras *c;* "calesero" (coachman); songs which used to be sung in the rhythm of the horse's hooves. In the style of the **Serrana,** but a little more cheerful. In the late 16th and early 17th centuries, people danced the **Caleseras** like the "Siguidillas." In 1922, however, in the "Concurso de Cante Jondo de Granada," they were classified as *libre*.

Campanilleros *c, t;* (bell-founder, bellringer). Folk songs in the *compás* of the **Fandanguillo,** often dealing with religious subjects. The **Campanilleros** were typical of MANUEL TORRE. Today they are only performed by the blind *cantaora* NIÑA DE LA PUEBLA. Major/minor and *modo dórico*.

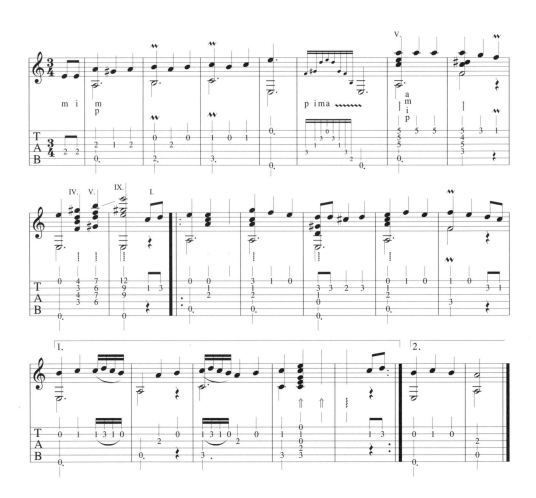

Cantiñas c, t; "cantiñear," "canturrear" (to hum along); a trimmed and very rhythmic **Alegría** in C-major. The word is also used as a generic term for **Alegrías, Romeras, Mirabrás** and **Caracoles.** See **Alegrías.**

Caña c, t, (b); according to ESTEBAN CALDERÓN'S "Escenas Andaluzas" (1847), **Caña** is derived from the Arabic word "gannia" (song). However, researchers claim that it derives from the Arabic words "ghana" or "anshada" (song). Another custom was "cantar a las cañas," i.e. "to sing to the glasses or to the wine glasses." The **Cañas** are sung in the *compás* of the **Soleá**. Before and after each *copla* the *lamento* "ay" is sung six times.

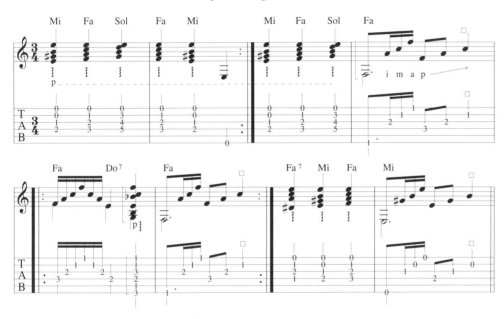

Cante de Galeras c; song of the galleys; its origin probably goes back to the 16th or 17th century. To be banished to the galleys – the fate of many *gitanos* – meant to face a slow death. So this kind of cante was performed accordingly. The tonality was free and the rhythm monotonous, in time with the strokes of the oars.

Caracoles c, t; traditional Andalusian song form, added to Flamenco in the mid 19th century. TÍO JOSÉ "EL GRANAÍNO" created the **Caracoles** and PACO "EL GANDUL" modified them by performing them in a livelier and more dynamic way. The great *cantaor* ANTONIO CHACON was a master of the **Caracoles** and made them popular in Madrid. The **Caracoles** belong to the group of the **Cantiñas.** In the *compás* of the **Alegrías,** mostly in do-major.

Carceleras c; Toná resembles the **Siguiriyas,** but *libre* and *a palo seco;* major mode; songs from the jails.

Cartagenera c; a kind of **Fandango,** with an *aire* resembling that of the **Tarantas.** At the end of the 19th century, the **Cartagenera,**

originally a folk song, was added to Flamenco. It belongs to the *cantes de levante*; *libre*; *modo dórico*.

Colombianas   *c, b, t;* influenced by Colombian folklore, similar to the "Habanera." Blend of **Guajiras** and **Rumba Gitana**. Made popular by CARMEN AMAYA and SABICAS, *cantes de ida y vuelta*. 2/4 time; major mode.

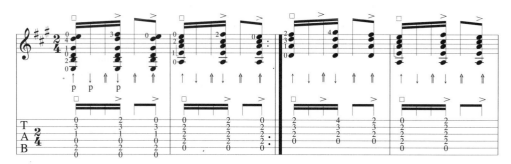

Corridas   *c;* or Corridos; *canción primitiva*. Probably one of the earliest song forms in Flamenco, derived from the "Romances Castellanos."

Chuflas   *c;* humorous, funny **Tanguillos** whose *coplas* are often only recited or performed as a kind of chant. They come from the Cadíz area and are performed best by the *gitanos*.

Danza Mora   *b, t;* Moorish dance; the dance, performed barefoot, is no longer in use nowadays. It resembles the **Zambra,** but is more serious and less sensual and includes slower movements of the arms without desplantes. Like most oriental dances, the **Danza Mora** is characterized by a mysterious sense of beauty.

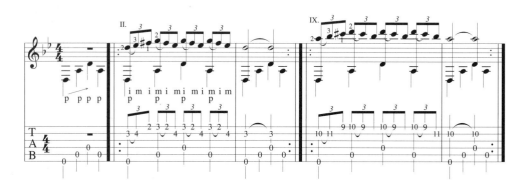

Debla	*c; Romaní* (goddess or virgin); like the **Toná,** but with religious contents and more difficult to sing. *A palo seco*, *libre*, in the *modo dórico*. In his book "Las Tonas Flamencas," the Flamencologist DON JOSÉ BLAS VEGA writes that the word **Debla** goes back to the *cantaor* BLAS BAREA who created this kind of **Tonás.** Since the Andalusians like to slur the last letters of a word, "de Blas Barea" turned into the nonce-word "de Bla."
Endecha	*c;* lament with a melancholic and painful expression. It has four lines with an assonance of six or seven syllables. One of the earliest primitive chants. No longer in use.
Fandangos	*c, t;* genre of the *cante andaluz*. In 1705, the word **Fandango** occurred in an etymological dictionary for the first time. In the early 16th century, some popular songs in Portugal were called "Esfandangos." The **Fandangos** belong to the very old Flamenco forms containing Arabic and northern Spanish elements.
	The **Fandango** exists in many variations today, bearing the names of great *cantaores* or of the region where they come from. They are divided into two main groups: "Fandango grande," including **Taranta** (*libre*) and **Taranto** (4/4 time), **Granaínas, Medias Granaínas, Malagueñas, Cartagenera** and **Mineras,** as well as "Fandaguillos," which are again divided into two categories: **Fandangos de Huelva** and **Fandangos de Málaga.** The **Fandangos** have no metrics (*libre*) and are pure *cantes*, except for the **Taranto.** The rhythm of the "Fandanguillos" is set in 3/4 time. The melody of the *coplas* is major and the last *tercio* ends on the dominant of the parallel minor key. The *coplas* consist of six *tercios,* with the first and third being identical.
Fandangos de Huelva	*c, b, t;* group or single dance from the region of Huelva, slightly varying from town to town. The most popular are the **Fandangos** de Alosno, Calañas, Encinasola, Puebla de Guzmán, Almonaster, El Cerro, Santa Barbara, Paymogo, Valverde and Villanueva. The *estribillo* is played in the *modo dórico*, the *coplas* in major, ending on the dominant of the parallel minor key. It is controversial whether the **Fandangos de Huelva** stem from the **Fandangos de Málaga** or the other way round. No difference can be found between the *compás* of the traditional-folkloric **Verdiales** and that of the **Fandangos de Huelva**. This becomes clear in the *estribillos* of the two *estilos*. The chord changes and

ESTILOS

number of bars are different, though (see **Volume I**, Fandangos de Huelva on page 109, **Verdiales**).

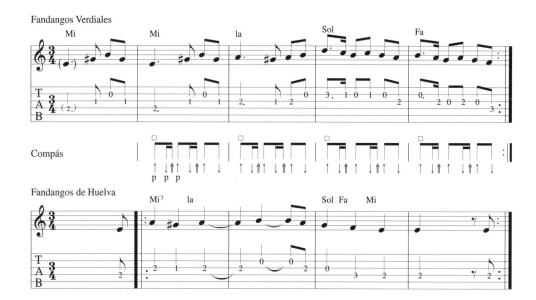

Fandangos de Málaga	*c, b, t;* **Verdiales, Rondeñas, Bandolás, Jabegotes, Jabera, Fandango** de Lucena, **Fandangos** de Almería, also called "*cantes* de abandolaos." Not all of them come from Málaga, but they all belong to this group. It is not clear whether they stem from the **Verdiales** or the **Rondeñas**.
Fandangos naturales	*c, t;* the guitar plays the same intro as in the **Fandangos de Huelva,** but the accompaniment of the *tercios* is *libre*.
Farruca	*c, b, t;* Asturian and Galician emigrants were called "farrucas" or "farrucos." In 1906 the dancers FAICO and RAMÓN MONTOYA modified this dance by using the *compás* of the **Tangos.** 4/4 time with a strong accent on 1 and a light accent on 3; in the minor mode.

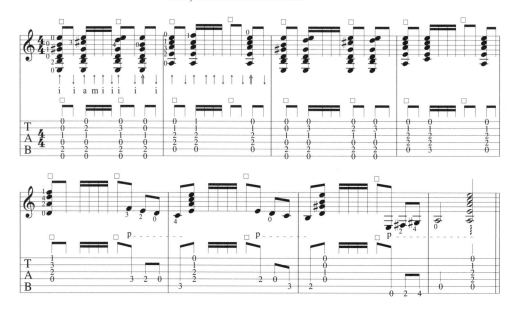

Garrotín   *c, b, t;* on the one hand, the **Garrotín** is said to have come from Asturia or Valladolid, on the other hand, it is said to have been created by the *gitanos* from Lérida and Tarragona. In the *compás* of the **Farruca;** usually in C-major or G-major (see **Volume I**, Lesson 3).

Granaínas   *c, t;* **Fandango** from Granada. The *tercios* of the **Granaínas** are slightly longer than those of the **Media Granaínas.** *Compás libre*, the melody in the *modo dórico*.

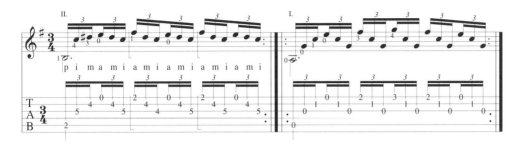

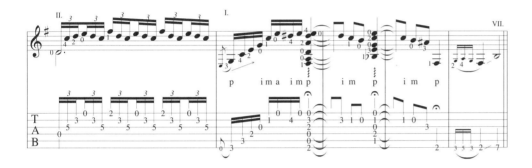

Guajiras   *c, b, t;* the white farmers in Cuba were originally called "guajiro." Later, the term was used for all farmers. This Cuban peasant song belongs to the *cantes de ida y vuelta*. In the major mode (mostly La-major).

ESTILOS

Jabegotas c, t; old form of the **Bandolás,** according to PEMARTÍN. "Cantes de los jabegotes," songs of the fishermen who were singing them while mending their "jábegas" (nets). Possibly also a derivative of **Jaberas.** In the *compás* of the **Verdiales.**

Jaberas c, t; the word is possibly derived from "la habera" (female bean seller) or from "jábega" (fishing net). The **Jaberas** belong to the group of **Fandangos de Málaga** or the **Verdiales.**

Jácara c; belongs to the *canciónes primitivas*. Song and dance form of the 16th century, derived from the **Romance.**

Jaleo(s) c, t; primitive form of the **Alegrías** and forerunner of the **Bulerías,** hardly ever performed nowadays. The *cante* is *airoso* and very rhythmic. The *coplas* include three *tercios*. The *tocaores* play the **Jaleo** in a rhythm which is a mixture of that of the **Bulerías** and the **Soleá por Bulerías.** In the *modo dórico*.

Jarchyas c; the song versifications of the "Seguidillas Castellanas" and the "Seguirillas Andaluzas" can be found in the Mozarabic **Jarchyas** from the 6th century. Belongs to the *canciónes primitivas*.

Livianas c; *cante* influenced by the **Toná;** sung in the *compás* of the **Siguiriyas** and **Serranas.** The **Livianas** was added to the category of the *cantes a palo seco* in 1922.

Malagueña c, t; **Fandango Grande** from the Malagá area. Great *cantaores* like ENRIQUE "EL MELLIZO", ANTONIO CHACON and JUAN BREVA created a *cante* with a strong melody, characterized by a profound deepness and solemnity. Tonality and rhythm are like those of the **Fandangos.** PEMARTÍN[1] believes that JUAN BREVA's **Malagueñas** are variations of the **Verdiales.** DE LA BRECHA[2] claims that the **Malagueñas** by "EL MELLIZO" and CHACON are not real **Malagueñas,** but that they originated in Alora and were made popular by EL CANARIO, EL PEROTE, LA RUBIA, LA TRINI and CAYETANO.

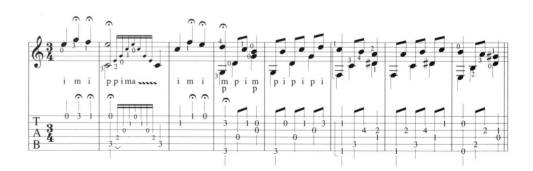

[1] Pemartín, Julian, Guía alfabética del Cante Flamenco
[2] Molina, R./Mairena, A., Mundos y formas del Cante Flamenco

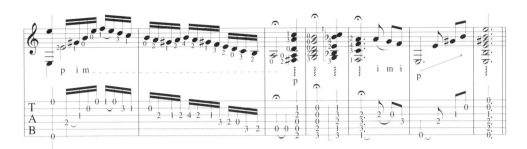

Marianas	*c, t;* "Cantes de los Zínganos" (gipsies from Hungary); NIÑO DE LOS MARIANAS was a specialist in this kind of *estilo* which was sung in the *compás* of the **Tientos** and is no longer in use nowadays.
Martinete	*c;* derives from the **Tonás** and probably originated in the gipsy smithies in Triana (martillo = hammer). It is sung in the *compás* of the **Siguiriyas** *a palo seco* in the *modo dórico* today. The *compás* is often beaten with the hammer on the anvil.
Media Granaína	*c, t;* the *tercios* are a little shorter and more Fandango-like than those of the **Granaína.**
Milonga	*c, t; cante de ida y vuelta;* originally from Argentinia. It is mainly sung in the *compás* of the **Rumba** today; minor mode and/or *modo dórico*.
Mineras	*c, t;* variation of the **Tarantas** from the Jaén and Murcia areas. The key is *Sol♯-dórico*, i.e. *Do♯-menor – Si – La – Sol♯*. Like the *copla* of the **Tarantas** or **Fandango,** the *copla* of the **Mineras** is accompanied in the major mode, i.e. in this case in *Mi-mayor,* and ends on *Sol♯7*.
Mirabrás	*c, b, t; cante* or *baile,* influenced by the **Alegrías.** The chords change from major to minor and back, often also to the *modo dórico*.
Nanas	*c;* lullabies; *a palo seco*, in the *modo dórico*.
Palmarés	*c;* old songs which used to be sung by the farm workers to the pace of the donkeys and oxen.
Peteneras	*c, b, t;* there are three hypotheses as far as their origin is concerned: 1. a religious *cante* of the *sefardís,* 2. they are

ESTILOS

similar to the "Punto de la Habana," and 3. the first **Petenera** was sung by a *cantaora* from Paterna, known as PATERNERA. Major/minor mode and *modo dórico*. Many *gitanos* take to their heels when they hear a **Petenera** because there is the superstition that it brings bad luck.

When I accompanied a **Petenera** singer for the first and last time, all Flamenco dresses, shoes and utensils belonging to the female dancers were stolen immediately after the concert. I had never been superstitious before.

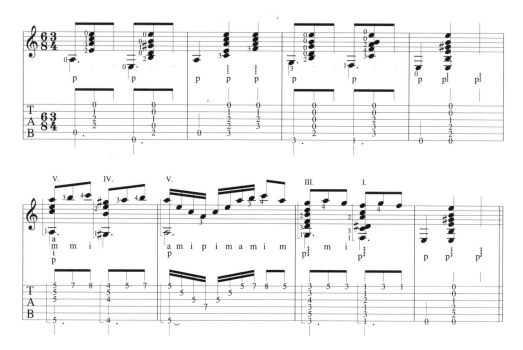

Plañidera c; *canción primitiva;* a woman crying at a grave was called "plañidera". Supposedly, the **Siguiriyas** developed from the **Plañidera** and the **Endecha**.

Playeras c; *cante primitiva;* again, there are two different opinions on the origin of the *cante:* 1. the **Playera** was a rhythmic song, accompanied with *palmas* and sung alternately by men and women. 2. The **Playera** is the predecessor of the **Siguiriyas**.

Polo c, t; an 18th century dance was called "El Polo." El Polo Flamenco was unknown until the 19th century; it originated from the **Caña**. The *coplas* consist of four *tercios* with eight syllables. The first *copla* is followed by the *lamentos*.

Pregón c; "Pregón" (public proclamation); the great *cantaor* MECANDÉ used the **Pregón** to sell his sweets in the street; *a palo seco*, major/minor mode and *modo dórico*. No longer in use.

Roas	*c, b;* a dance imported from the orient by the *gitanos*. The women formed a circle and the men played tambourine. No longer in use. The arm and body movements are reminiscent of an ancient ritual of religious origin.
Romance	*c;* or Romanza, belongs to the *canciones primitivas*. Poetic songs whose verses consist of eight syllables.
Romeras	*c, b, t;* a danceable form of the **Cantiñas.** ROMERO EL TITO invented this *cante,* to which one can also dance and which was named after him, using an old **Cantiña.**
Rondeñas	*c, t;* like the **Verdiales,** but with a less prominent rhythm, from the mountainous region of Ronda.
Rondeña	*t;* RAMÓN MONTOYA composed his legendary Rondeña with ⑥ tuned to re and ③ tuned to fa♯. This beautiful composition has nothing in common with the **Rondeñas**. It is a reminiscence of the mountainous region around Ronda. The **Rondeña** was performed as a solo dance by CARMEN AMAYA, LUISA MARAVILLA and MANUELA CARRASCO, with the *compás* and *toque* resembling the **Taranto.** Below is a shortened intro and an *ayudado-falseta* of the "Toque Rondeña."

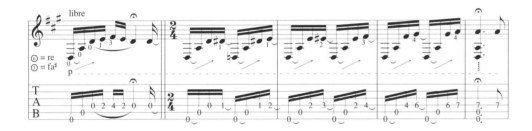

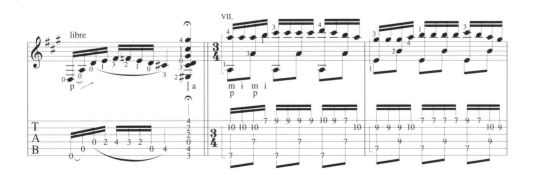

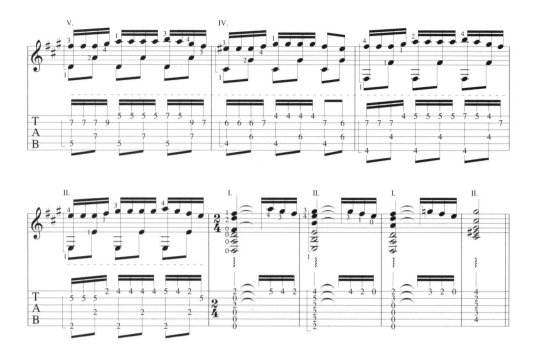

Rumba	*c, b, t; cantes de ida y vuelta;* **Rumba** flamenca: *modo dórico;* **Rumba** aflamenca: major/minor mode and *modo dórico;* **Rumba** concretamenta: major/minor mode. Although the **Rumba** has become very popular recently, purists don't appreciate it very much and don't acknowledge it as belonging to Flamenco. On the other hand, it is probably impossible to learn to perform the **Rumba** like the *gitanos* do. See **Volume I,** Lessons 2 and 3.
Saetas	*c; cantes* which are mainly sung during the *Semana Santa*. Probably of Jewish origin. Strongly influenced by the **Martinetes.** In the *compás* of the **Siguiriyas** or the **Martinetes;** *a palo seco* or with drum and trumpet accompaniment. The lyrics deal with Christ's Passion and the grief of the Virgin Mary.
Serranas	*c, t;* in the 19th century Flamenco jargon „serrana" meant gitana. Mountain dwellers were also called „serranos." Originally, the **Serrana** was a folk song and was „flamencocized" in the mid 19th century. In the *modo dórico,* but mostly *por arriba;* begins on 8 like the **Siguiriyas.**
Sevillanas	*c, b, t;* folkloric pair-dance derived from the „Seguidillas Manchegas." Every **Sevillanas** – people always sing or dance four of them – consists of an *introducción* (guitar, 8 bars), *salida* (singer, 6 bars) and *copla* (12 bars: 9 bars melody, 3 bars guitar) which is sung three times. It is accompanied in ³/₄ time, but many **Sevillanas** are sung in ²/₄ time, the time preferred for dancing. The **Sevillanas** are divided into the following groups: „Sevillanas Boleras" (in the style of the songs performed at court); „Sevillanas bíblicas" and „Sevillanas corraleras" (dealing with biblical and rural subjects); „Sevillanas rocieras," sung at the „Romería (pilgrim-

age) de la Virgen del Rocío" with drum accompaniment. See **Volume I,** Lesson 4.

Siguiriyas *c, b, t;* derived from the **Playeras** and **Endechas** and influenced by the **Plañideras.** The *gitanos* aligned and extended this *cante*. In his „Antología Flamenco", DOMINGO JOSÉ SAMPERIO pointed out that the word is of Indian and gipsy origin. The **Siguiriyas** is the most emotional *cante*. Its rhythm is not always metrical because the *melismas* are often extended and the syllables are sung *rubato*. In the *modo dórico*. Begins on the 8 of the *reloj*. Only in the 20th century did people begin to dance the **Siguiriyas.**

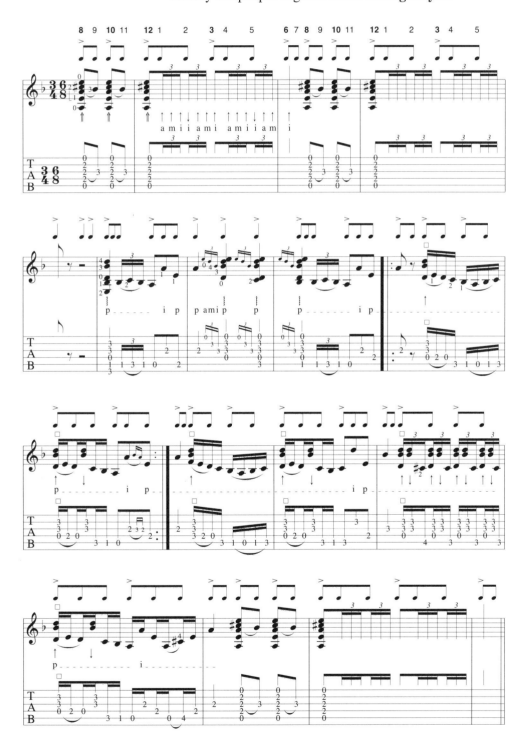

ESTILOS

Soleá — *c, b, t;* or **Soleares;** originally a 16th century *cante* called „Soleades" (loneliness), which was gradually modified by countless *cantaores* until it achieved its modern form. The *gitanos* had already played **Soleás** before they first appeared in Triana in 1840. The most important "estilos por Soleá" are those from Triana, Alcalá, Utrera, Jerez, Cádiz and Córdoba. Begins on 1. **Soleá** grande: four-line *coplas* whose *tercios* are longer and more difficult to sing; **Soleá** corta: three-line *coplas;* Soleariya: three-line *coplas,* but with a shorter first line. See **Volume I**, Lessons 2, 3, 4 and **Volume II**, Lessons 6, 10.

Soleá por Bulerías — *c, b, t;* often called "Soleá por medio." The term is also used for a **Soleá** in La-dórico. The **Soleá por Bulerías** resembles the early *estilos* of the **Bulerías** and only differs from the **Soleá** in the rhythm, which is basically in the *compás* of the **Alegrías.**

Tangos — *c, b, t;* one of the oldest *cantes gitanos* whose origin is in dispute. According to the oral tradition of the *gitanos*, **Tangos** have always been sung in Triana. The most important **Tangos** are those of Triana, Málaga (Tangos de Piyayo), Cádiz, Jerez (Frijones) and the "Tangos Canastero" (a canastero is a nomadic gitano). Straight rhythm in 4/4 time with a strong accent on the 1 and 3. See **Volume I**, Lessons 1, 2, 3, 4 and **Volume II**, Lesson 10.

Tanguillos — *c, b, t;* a blend of **Tangos** and **Rumba,** mainly performed by Gaditanos (inhabitants of Cádiz). "Las Murgas" is a group of several singers who sing only **Tanguillos.** The *compás* is beaten on a pitcher a with a raffia shoe.

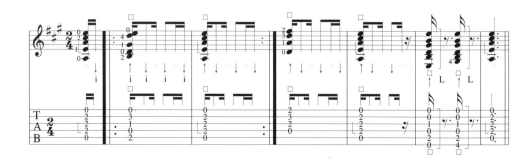

Tarantas — *c, b, t;* belongs to the group of *cantes de levante* (south-east coast of Spain). Developed from the **Fandangos,** but is played in a straight, unmetrical time. Mostly deals with subjects concerning the miners. *Si-dórico (Si – La – Sol – Fa♯).*

Taranto — *c, b, t;* danceable form of the **Tarantas** (4/4 time) in the *compás* of the **Zambra.** Majestic and *jondo.* See **Volume I**, Lesson 3 and **Volume II**, Lessons 6, 10.

Temporeras *c;* no longer in use. A kind of **Fandango** with its supposed origin in Cabra (Córdoba). The **Temporeras** were performed *a palo seco* by several singers, each one singing a *copla*.

Tientos *c, b, t;* this *cante* was imported by the first *gitanos* who settled down in Spain. It was accompanied with the Indian "tamboura." According to another theory, the word is derived from "tandear" (to try), explaining that this *cante* was the predecessor of the stricter and more rhythmic **Tangos.**

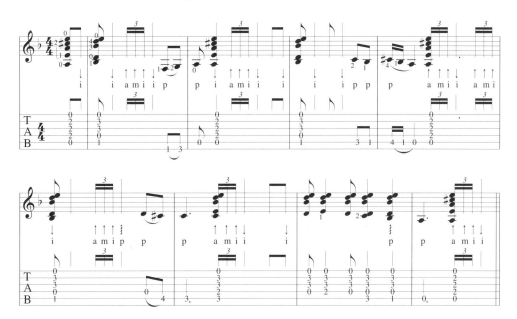

Toná *c;* the word comes from "tonada" (song, tune) and first appeared in 1611. The Flamenco-**Toná** was first mentioned in 1847. Was sung *a palo seco* and *libre*, but fell into total oblivion. The street singers carried the **Tonás** from village to village.

Verdiales *c, t;* there are different theories about the origin of the word. One of them says that the **Verdiales** were named after a small town near Málaga. Another theory refers to an olive cultivation area in the province of Málaga or to a variety of olive of the same name. The **Verdiales** belong to the oldest **Fandangos** of Andalusia. These **Fandangos** are called "fiestas" by the rural population. They are traditionally accompanied with violin, tambourine, *bandurria, bandola* or *laúd* and *castañuelas* during the *ferias* in Málaga. The instrumentation, which is typical of a North African orchestration, points to their Moorish origin. As a contrast, the dance includes northern Spanish elements (abrupt movements, no *taconeos* and shoes with soft soles) like the *jota*. The **Verdiales** are danced individually, in pairs or in a group of three – two women and one man. The dancer is called "zángano" and must never turn his back on the women. There are three different types of **Verdiales:** The old, simple dance form with a strong rhythm.

ESTILOS

The more flexible and extended form consisting only of *cantes*. A less known form from the area around Córdoba (Baena and Puente Genil) and Antequera, with a melancholy tone like the **Fandangos** de Lucena. The **Fandangos** de Los Lagares, **Zángano** de Puente Genil, La **Rondeña** and La **Jabera, Bandolás** and **Jabegotes** are all in the *compás* of the **Verdiales.**

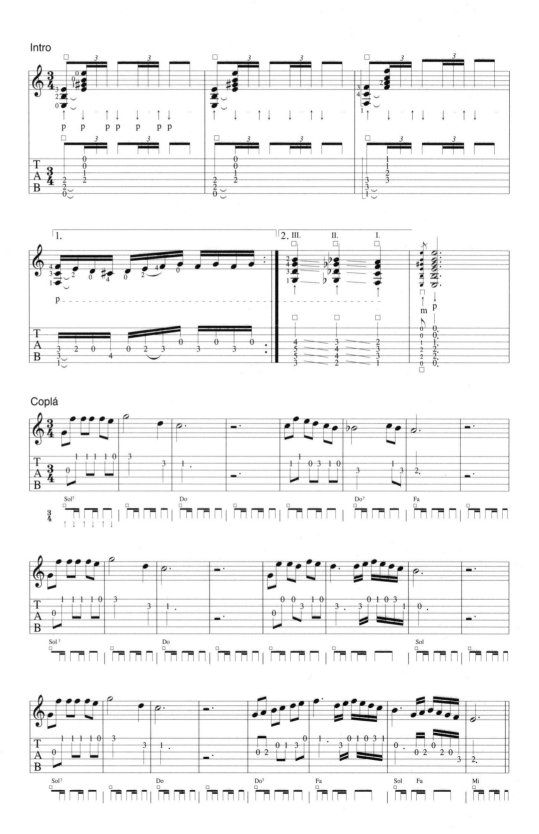

Villancico *c, t;* folkloric Christmas carols.

Zambra *b, t;* originally a Moorish dance. Derived from "zampra" (Arabic: flute); in the *compás* of the **Tangos;** was mainly performed by the *gitanos* of the "Sacro Monte" (mountain in Granada with gipsy caves; now a tourist attraction).

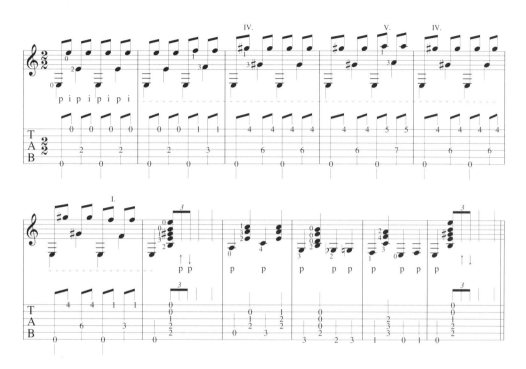

Zapateado *b, t;* or Zapateado Catalan; probably comes from the "Zapateado del Monte" (Guajiro dance from Cuba) and the **Zarandillo.** Originally a male dance, nowadays it is also performed by women with the *traje corto* and the *córdobes*. The *compás* is like that of the **Tanguillo,** 6/8 or 2/4 time, mostly in *Do-mayor*.

ESTILOS

Zarandillo c, b; folkloric song and dance form, probably derived from the Sarabande. Its rhythm consists of alternating 6/8 and 3/4 times, like the **Guajiras.** No longer in use.

Zorongo Gitano c, b, t; FEDERÍCO GARCIA LORCA rediscovered this old Flamenco form, adding lyrics and a melody. The rhythm changes from slow 3/4 time to the fast Bulerías-*compás*.

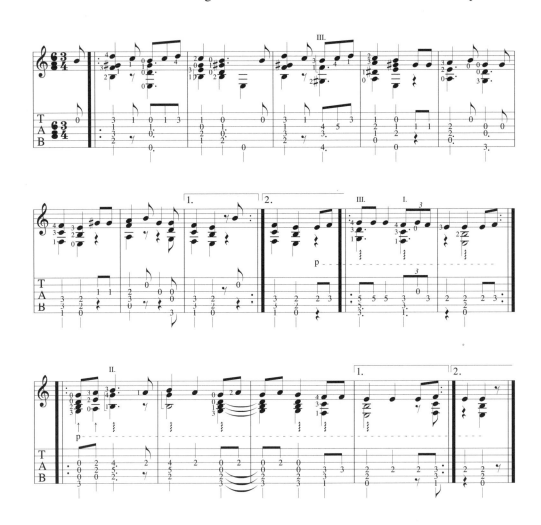

HISTORY

- Introduction
- Antiquity
- Middle Ages
- The Moors
- The Reconquista
- The Jews
- The Inquisition
- The Conquista
- The Gipsies
- Terminology
- Development of Flamenco
- Flamenco in the 50s and Today
- Los Tablaos
- El Cante – El Baile – El Toque
- Pasión

The 15 regions of the Spanish mainland and the Balearic Islands

History

Introduction

The development of this musical phenomenon is based on a variety of cultural influences, social tensions and the exclusion of ethnic groups such as gipsies, Jews and Moors in southern Spain. Finding the origins of Flamenco is difficult, since there are only very few written records from past centuries. To investigate its early roots it is necessary to explore the cultural history of Andalusia and the different musical elements in Flamenco which point to its varied origins. Thanks to this blend of different musical origins, Flamenco has become what it is today: fascinating and at the same time eluding detailed analysis. Even flamencologists often disagree and have no choice but to rely on guesswork. Often, the only way to form your own opinion is to decide whether to believe more in the works of one author than in those of another. There is no standard theory about Flamenco, only descriptions of different opinions which are full of contradictions.

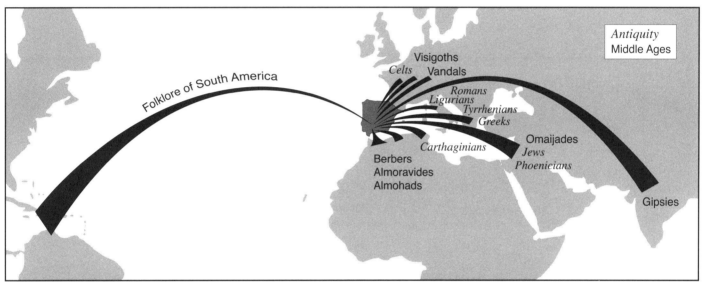

Direct and indirect cultural influences

Nobody can say exactly when Flamenco began. However, we can suppose that, long before Flamenco as such became known, a folklore existed in Andalusia, whose elements were rooted in Flamenco. The very term *modo dórico*, which is often used in these two volumes, is a reason for tracing its history back to this area.

Antiquity

The Bronze Age cave paintings in Andalusia, such as "La Pileta" near Ronda (25,000 to 30,000 years old), or the "Cultura Almeriense" (ceramic and copper art) from "Los Miralles" near Almería, prove that works of art have been created on the Iberian Peninsula since the Ice Age. Because music, or dance, is an older form of art than painting, we may assume that the origins of one of the most original and richest forms of music in the world go back to that time.

The first tribes we know of were the Iberians, pre-Indo-Europeans who probably came from northern Africa and settled down in the south and east. They had fortified towns and a writing system (stone monuments, lead tablets, coins and ceramics); the

HISTORY

Ligurians, non-Indo-Europeans native to the south of France, northern Italy and the Western Alps; the Tyrrhenians, an Etruscan[1] tribe, who built the legendary wealthy trading city of Tartessos (Tarsis, biblical name: Tarschisch) on an island – which later sank in the sea – in the river delta of the Guadalquivir. As early as between 2500 and 1700 B.C. there were contacts between the Iberians in Andalusia and Britanny, the British Isles, Scandinavia and Germania. Later, around 1200, relations between Iberian Spain and southern Italy were established.

In 1100 B.C. the first settlers, the Phoenicians, came from the Eastern Mediterranean. They were the first Mediterranean seafarers to venture out of the Strait of Gibraltar where they built a trading port and called it Gadir (today Cádiz) in honour of Neptune's son. Apart from commodities, they also brought musical instruments such as the "kinnor" (portable harp) and crotales (antique cymbals) made of metal.

The Jews probably came with the Phoenicians. According to the findings of IS D ABBOUS[2], the era of the Jews began long before the Christian era. This assumption is shared by SIMON WIESENTHAL[3] who further found out that the names of the cities of Toledo, Maqueda, Escalona, Joppes and Aceca suggest Palestinian-Jewish origins and sound Hebrew (See "Jews," page 120).

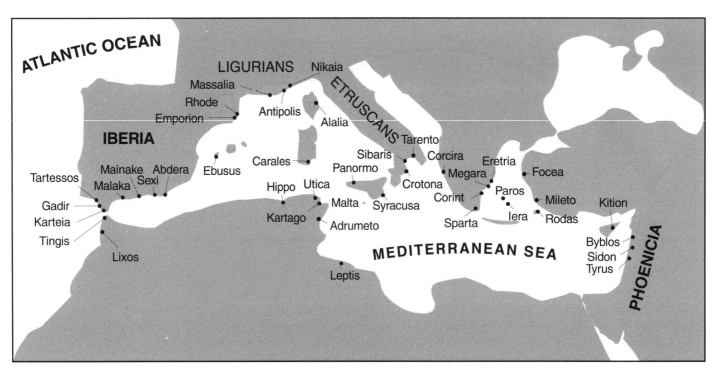

Phoenician and Greek settlements

Around 800 B.C., the Greek, well-known seafarers, arrived. They established many colonies, not only along the coastline, but also in the interior, and left numerous architectural and cultural treasures. The origin of the Spanish dances goes back to that time. You can see lively female dancers, turning and swinging, on bowls, pitchers and plates. Strict Greeks like Plato and Aristide despised these dissipated and unbridled dances and chants which had been performed in a similar manner in distant Phoenicia long before. We owe the name "Iberia," derived from a river called Iber (probably to-

---

1 Latin: Etrusci, Tusci; Greek: Tyhrrhenoi, Tyrsenoi; important people in ancient Italy
2 Musulmans Andalous et Judéo-Espagnols
3 Segel der Hoffnung (Walter-Verlag, Olten)

day's Tinto) to the Greeks. Only much later was the name Iber assigned to the river Ebro.

Since the Greeks developed their music theory much later, it could be true that the *modo dórico* was imported to Hellas from the south of Spain.

The Celts, too, ventured as far as Spain. Their first invasion in the north-east around 900 B.C. was followed by a second invasion in the north-west and east from 600 B.C. They merged with the Iberians and were called Celtiberians. It was presumably at that time that the Celts received the valuable gift of the alphabet which had existed in Iberia for some time. The old-Celtic bards can be compared with the Greek Rhapsodes[4]. Being poets and singers, they formed a class of high repute. They accompanied themselves, first with the crwth, a lyre-like stringed instrument, later with the frame harp. While Celtic culture was in keeping with the cold and damp north-west of the European Iron Age, Iberian culture experienced its heyday in the pleasant climate of the south under oriental influences.

The "relatives" of the Phoenicians, the Carthaginians, who came from North Africa (today's Tunis), were not as friendly as the Phoenicians. They penetrated further into the interior than the previous colonists. Around 535 B.C. they destroyed Tartessos. They traded, but preferred to strengthen their military position of power. The Carthaginians founded cities like "Barcino" (Barcelona) and "Carthago Nova" (Cartagena).

The population of southern Iberia lived a secluded life in its own culture, cut off from the orient by the Carthaginian blockade, until the Romans came. Their civilisation was so highly developed that even laws were put into verse and sung. When the Romans expelled the Carthaginians from the southern and eastern regions in 200 B.C., important trading and cultural cities like Cádiz, Sevilla, Córdoba, Málaga and Cartagena had long been established. That is why romanization had a stronger and more lasting impact than on other peoples on the Iberian Peninsula. Whereas the Iberians in the south were used to foreign occupying forces and obsequiously accepted the Roman rulers, the conquest of the rest of Spain took the Romans a further two hundred years of battle. By the time the whole country was subject to the same rules and language, the Andalusians had already been civilised and romanized for two centuries, speaking Latin and using it for the verses of their songs. The Greek music systems, imported by the Romans, were also well-known.

During 600 years of Roman rule, "Hispania" was a Roman vassal state whose art was of high international repute. Soon there were writers and philosophers, even emperors, who were Romans at heart and as far as citizenship was concerned, but whose birthplaces were in Spain. The Spanish epigram writer MARCUS VALERIUS MARTIALIS[5] wrote about the sensual and seductive dances of the girls from Gades (Cádiz) who enchanted the Roman society with the movements of their feet and the crotales on their fingers. DECIMUS IUNIUS IUVENALIS[6] claimed that these dancers "were murmuring love chants from Baetica." You can still hear this murmur, or soft singing, today, especially when listening to the cantaores of the cante jondo.

Middle Ages

After the decline of power of the West-Roman Empire (from about 400 A.D.) the Vandals (an East-Germanic tribe) passed through and looted Spain. However, after a short time they were driven to North Africa by the Visigoths where they established an

---

4 travelling bards
5 (about 40-102 A.D.)
6 (about 60-127 A.D.), Roman satirist

HISTORY

up-and-coming empire around Carthage (429-534). Two hundred years later, the Moors named Andalusia after them: "Al-Andalus" (Vandalusia).

Between 409 and 429 A.D. the Visigoths conquered Spain from the north. These belligerent Barbarians, who stayed in the country for about 300 years, left no cultural or social traces. The only event was the introduction of the Christian religion (587) as the state religion. Due to the shortcomings of the Visigothic military regime, the south of Spain was left with its usual task of developing its culture and civilisation itself. During that period, a light was shining in Sevilla, not only for Spain, but for all of Christendom: ST. ISIDOR[7].

The Moors

In 711 A.D. seven thousand Berbers led by the Arab commander and governor of Tanger, TARIK IBU ZAYAD, crossed the Strait of Gibraltar[8]. The *moros* were allegedly

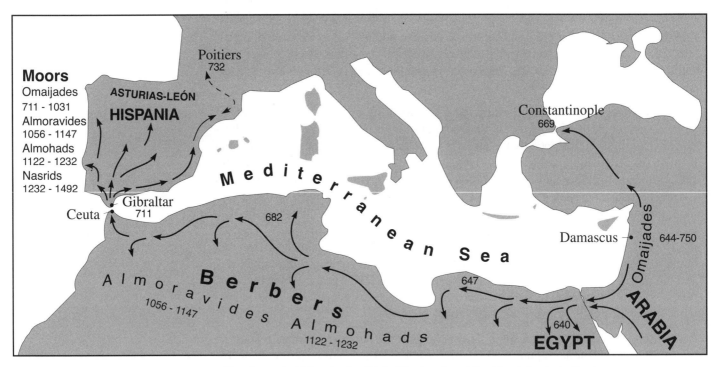

The Spread of Islam by the "Holy Warriors," and the Moorish rule in Spain

called by COUNT JULIAN to revenge his daughter who had been abducted by the Gothic king RODRIGO (Roderic). After the first successful battle near Jerez de la Frontera, an estimated 200,000 moros followed in a second large wave. They were Berbers from what is today Libya, Tunesia, Algeria, Morocco and Mauritania and, who, like the Egyptians, were islamized and ruled by the Arabs during the 7th century. Their Arab army commanders, mainly Syrians and Yemenis, were under the control of the caliphate of Damascus. The new rulers met only with little resistance because neither an organized nor a centralized state existed. In addition, they ruled by means of contracts guaranteeing their partners quite a lot of independence on payment of protection money, and they never touched what was dearest to the people of Hispania: their religion.

---

7 (about 560-636) Archbishop of Sevilla, conveyed ancient and old Christian cultural assets, established the basics of the Mozarabic liturgy and summarized the entire dogmatics and morals in his "Book of Maxims."
8 Gib (Jebel) al Tar = rock, or mountain, of Tarik

After the first quarrels between Berbers and Arabs, ABD AL RAHMAN, who came from the caliphate of Damascus and belonged to the House of Omaimjades, was proclaimed Emir of Al-Andalus in "La Mezquita," the mosque of Córdoba, in 788. Under his successor, ABD AL RAHMAN II, the Córdoban Caliphate was founded. Córdoba became the centre of science, research, literature and music and attracted students from all over Europe. The Arabs sent for musicians, dancers and musical instruments (for instance the *laúd*) from Damascus, Baghdad and Medina. Formerly unknown agricultural crops such as rice, sugarcane (before, only honey had been used as a sweetener throughout Europe), lemons and apricots were cultivated, and huge flocks of sheep supplied the weavers with plenty of wool. Remarkable irrigation plants were built, some of which are still beneficial to Spanish agriculture. The Arabs were masters of trades such as paper manufacturing, cloth weaving, metal and leather processing and ceramics. In the 10th century, Córdoba had eighty state schools, many public libraries, universities,

The Alhambra with the Sierra Nevada in the background

baths and hospitals. In mathematics, the decimal system including the zero was introduced; before that, only the Roman numerals had been known. In medicine, knowledge about anatomy and autopsy as well as the healing power of herbs and toxins was acquired. The first pharmacies were established in Andalusia. Palaces and mosques with beautiful gardens were built, which are still regarded as wonders of architecture. Moorish Spain gradually developed into one of the wealthiest and most populous European countries with an incredible mixture of people with different ways of life. Arabs, Berbers, Moors, Jews and Spaniards lived together in different quarters, and the courts were dominated by the luxurious and lascivious lives of the oriental rulers. The upper classes spoke Arabic, whereas the masses spoke the so-called "Romance" (Roman-Spanish). In the whole of Andalusia, especially in Córdoba, a diverse cultural life was developing. Liturgic music in the synagogue; Greek, Byzantine, Muslim and Jewish chants and tunes from Persia, Iraq and North Africa mixed with local songs and music. A musician worth mentioning was the founder of the National Academy of Music, Zyriab, who probably came from Iraq. He was said to be able to play more than ten thousand tunes and was an excellent lutenist. He exchanged the silk strings for lion gut strings and added a fifth string to the *laúd,* which had previously had only four strings.

In 929 ABD AL RAHMAN III proclaimed himself caliph of "Al Andalus." By 1031, when the caliphate was abolished and Muslim Spain broke up into several autonomous "taifas" (Arabic petty kingdoms), he had had fourteen successors. During the Christian counter-offensive the Almoravides (Al-Murabit = belligerent monks, or religious warriors) came to power and were overthrown by the Almohades (Al-Muwahhid = uniter) in 1146. In their religious fanaticism (they knew more about swords than books) they even destroyed their own co-religionists' works of art. The Nasrids

HISTORY

"Patio de los Leones" in the Alhambra

(1238-1492) were the last Moorish rulers. Despite being vassals of King FERDINAND III, they founded the Kingdom of Granada with Arabic diplomacy and without sabre-rattling, and succeeded in holding it until the end of the Reconquest (1492). During this final phase, after all kingdoms had been reconquered by the Christians, many Moorish refugees went to Granada and contributed to the final heyday of Islamic culture. In contrast to Córdoba as the occidental centre of science, Granada was the centre of the fine arts, music, literature and architecture. The Alhambra, an architectural marvel, was extended and enhanced.

The Reconquest (Reconquista)

The Reconquest, i.e. the reconquering of Spain from the Moors, and the Conquista, i.e. the conquest of America, began in 1492 and are still celebrated as national events today. The Reconquest began as early as eleven years after Rodrigo's defeat by the Visigothic king PEALYO at the battle of Covadonga Valley (Asturian mountains) near Jerez. Pealyo's victory led to the establishment of the kingdom of Asturia-León. According to the historian Menéndez Pidal, there are three well-defined epochs of the Reconquest. The first lasted from 720 to 1002. In Asturia and Catalonia, resistance groups formed, the river Ebro being their natural border. From 1045 to 1250, a great offensive was taken; Alfons VI captured Toledo, El Cid took Valencia, and Sevilla was recaptured in 1248. In the third epoch, the Christians profited from the quarrels between Moors of different race and religion and the fragmentation into small "taifas." However, the conquerors, too, were held up because of battles between the Christian rulers and the battle of the Spanish aristocracy against the king. When Granada was surrendered to the "Reyes Católicos," ISABELLA OF CASTILE and FERDINAND II OF ARAGÓN, in 1492, however, the last glorious kingdom of the Moors came to an end and made way for the unity of the Spanish kingdom. The surrender took place in a small town called Santa Fé near Granada which has henceforth been called "la cuna de la Hispaniadad" (the cradle of Spanish unity).

The Jews

As mentioned before, the Jewish epoch began long before the Christian era. This allegation is substantiated by the fact that, in Christ's day, Jewish pilgrims called "sephardim" came from Spain to Jerusalem. "Sepharad" (the biblical term) denoted the western country in the Mediterranean Sea, i.e. Spain. Also, many Jews came to Spain together with the Roman legions.

In the first centuries A.D., the Jews lived in perfect harmony with the partly pagan and partly christianized population. They were well-liked because of their manual skills and mental agility. Under the Visigothic kings they were granted equal rights as well. This changed, however, when King Recared I converted to Catholicism at the end of the 6th century. During the reign of the last Gothic kings the Jews lived in uncertainty: laws were passed and abolished again. Many Jews fled to Africa or were baptized. Their uncertainty ended with the invasion of the Moors. The Jews welcomed the conquerors as their liberators, and the gates of many a town, especially in the south, opened virtually of their own accord. The heyday of the Jews in Spain was between the 9th and 12th century, during the reign of the Omaijades. The Moorish rulers appreciated the usefulness of the Jews. They entrusted them with the organisation of business life and, because of their talent for languages, with the diplomatic relations. Since they were familiar with classical literature and Greek philosophy, the Jewish scholars were held in high esteem by the Moors. The most eminent Jewish genius at that time was Moses Maimonides. His work, "The Guide of the Perplexed," written in Arabic, appeared around 1190 and was of exceptional importance to medieval philosophy. However, this changed completely when the fanatic, strict and belligerent Almohades took over. Many Jews fled to the Christian north where they could move about freely, others helped the Christians with the Reconquista. Like the Moors, the *sefardís,* as the Jews are called in Spain, who had influenced life in Spain for centuries, were expelled by a decree issued by the REYES CATÓLICOS in 1478.

The Inquisition

When FERDINAND and ISABELLA, Kings of Castile, decided to "cleanse" Spain of minorities in an endeavour for racial purity and religious unity (Catholicism being the only religion), a sad process began, depriving Spain of some of the important representatives of its cultural, economic and academic life. Thousands of Jews and Muslims escaped, those who stayed behind were forced to be baptized. The Moors, still needed because of their knowledge, were promised religious freedom at first, but were later baptized by force *(moriscos)* as well and expelled from the country once and for all after a rebellion in 1569. In 1491 the first stakes, called "autodafés," were burning in Sevilla. Heretics, witches, people of different religions, mainly Muslims and Jews, later also gipsies, were sentenced to death. After torturing them to make them confess, the method of "killing without bloodshed" was employed: the flame was regarded as the holy instrument of purification. FRANCISCO JIMENEZ DE CISNEROS, first a Franciscan friar, later cardinal of Toledo, spread the Inquisition as far as Africa and America. In an interview on the subject, FREDERICO GARCIA LORCA[9] said, "Spain lost an admirable civilisation, a poetry, an architecture, an astronomy and an exquisiteness that were unique in the world."

The influence of the Jews on Flamenco can be traced back to that time. The Jews who renounced their faith, called conversos, continued their rituals and customs among themselves. They sang **Saetas**, closely related with the liturgical chants in the synagogues, to communicate with each other. The **Saeta** might have its origin in the Kol-Nidre prayer in which the sefardís ask God to annul the oath they had sworn to the Catholic Church.

> "If people say that without torture and prisons, Flamenco will cease to exist, then I will say: no! People will always have emotions like joy and pain. The names, the monuments may change, but everything else will stay the same."

Pepe el de la Matrona (cantaor)

---

[9] 1898-1936, lyric poet and playwright, was shot by Francoists, together with Manuel de Falla. Organised the first "Concurso de Cante jondo" in Granada (1922).

The Conquista

The Conquista (conquest) was the epoch in which Spain rose to world power because of its conquest of the "New World" and other countries. The famous "conquistadores," Cortez and Pizarro, conquered the Aztec (Mexico, 1521) and Inca (Peru, 1531) empires employing cruel methods. This era, helping Spain to wealth and power, was called "Siglo de Oro" (Golden Age). The whole of Europe was impressed by Spain's glory under Charles V and his son Philip II. The Spanish court etiquette served as a model to all royal courts. However, during the reign of Philip II[10] the empire already began to totter: there were wars against France and Italy, the break with the Netherlands and the defeat of the Armada. Spain's world power ended with the death of Philip II.

The Thirty Years' War, the Spanish wars of succession, the War of Independence started by Napoleon, the Civil War under Franco and the transition to democracy in 1976 were of no cultural importance, compared with the former history of the country.

The Gipsies

India is the presumed country of origin of the gipsies. However, to date, researchers have not been able to prove whether they came from the valleys of the Indus (more than three thousand kilometres long) or Rajasthan (a state bordering Pakistan) or the Hindukusch mountains. And it is not quite clear, either, why they left their native

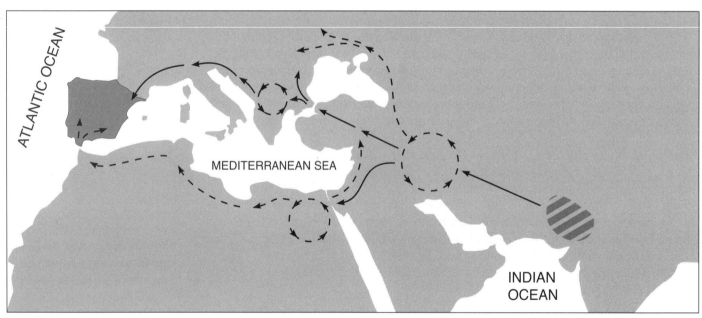

Migration of the gipsies to Spain

country in the 7th, 8th or 10th century A.D. There are different hypotheses which do not exclude each other. The gipsies went to the west, following the setting sun, passed through Persia, where they probably stayed for a while, as is proved by the many Persian words in *romaní*, the Gipsy language, passed through Turkey, or possibly also came to Europe from the north of the Black Sea. The first gipsies reached the Balkans in the middle of the 14th century. It can be proved that the first gipsies arrived in

---

10 1500-1558; 1516: Spanish king; 1519-1556: German king and Roman emperor; from the House of Habsburg, son of Philip the Handsome of Austria and Juana la Loca (Joana the Mad), daughter of the Reyes Católicos

Germany in 1417, in Italy (Bologna) in 1422, in France (Paris) in 1427 and in Spain (Jaca, Navarra) in 1425. The gipsies are called "gitanes" in French and *gitanos* (egipcianos) in Spanish. The origin of the words goes back to the fact that the gipsies called themselves Egyptians or claimed they were pilgrims from Egypt Minor – but it is unclear what they meant by that. For this reason, many reference books still claim that the Andalusian gitanos came to Spain via Egypt and North Africa. I'd like to add another hypothesis: if the gipsies had actually been in Egypt, there was only one possibility for their basic instinct to follow the setting sun, and that was to travel along the Mediterranean coast of North Africa.

At first, like in many other countries, the gipsies were met with a warm reception in Spain, because they posed as pilgrims. A document dating from 1425 was found in Barcelona, a letter of safe-conduct, issued by KING ALFONSO V to JUAN DE EGIPTO MENOR, saying that these pilgrims must be treated well and should be allowed to go on their way. As early as in 1499, a decree was issued by the REYES CATÓLICOS which marked the beginning of the expulsion and persecution of the gipsies. FELIX GRANDE[11] quotes the entire contents of the decree. Here is a loosely translated excerpt: "The gipsies must not hang around in the country in future. They must leave the country within sixty days. Anyone who does not obey this rule will get one hundred blows with a stick. The second time, his ears will be cut off and he will be given a dungeon sentence of sixty days. The third time, he shall be stuck in the dungeon for life." In the 16th century, the gipsies were forbidden to speak their language, to use their names and to wear their clothes. When they refused to be baptized, they were threatened by the Inquisition. Many gipsies escaped to the rough regions in the mountains where they lived from smuggling and occasional thefts, others had to give up their nomadic existence and were forced to settle down in cities with more than 1,000 families. Most of those *gitanerías* were found in the poor district of the cities.

As late as under CARLOS III[12] the gipsies were granted a certain equality, at least according to the law. Although this didn't solve the problem of isolation and discrimination, they could at least be sure that they were no longer persecuted. Still, they were severely punished for the most trivial offences. They banded closely together and mostly kept to themselves.

Many *gitanos* settled in Andalusia because they liked the climate and had the possibility of finding work, mostly in the ports. Another reason might have been the cultural similarities between the gipsies and the Andalusians, as FELIX GRANDE men-

View from the Alhambra to the Sacro Monte

---
11 Felix Grande, Memoria del Flamenco
12 Charles III, 1759-1788 from the House of Bourbon, a reform zealous monarch.

HISTORY

> **Gipsy Saga**
>
> After God had created the earth he formed a human being from clay in His own image and put him in the oven. His first attempt was unsuccessful, the human being was too dark, and He said to him, "You shall live in the hot south." With the second one, God was overcautious and opened the oven door too early. The result was a pale creature that hadn't baked long enough. "You shall live in the cool north so that your skin won't get burned by the sun." The third time He opened the oven door at the right time. A successful human being came out, nicely bronzed. God was satisfied and spoke, "The black man lives in the south where he is not cold, the white one lives in the north where the sun is not so hot, and you, gipsy, are free to travel around in the whole wide world."

> Pupelé on Chal,
>
> ta saró sundache sina men chiquén, presas sino aotal.
>
> I was born in Egypt, and the whole world is my home because that is where I come from.

Caló texts from José Carlos de Luna, Los Gitanos de la Bética.

tions. The gipsies were much better off in Andalusia than elsewhere. Here, they were at least tolerated by the authorities and people. The country with its extensive olive groves, lush vineyards, forests and rivers looked like paradise. However, the people lived in great poverty because in this paradise, which had been taken away from the Moors and Jews, 2% of the population owned 90% of the land. The few people who did have work were low-paid and treated badly by the upper class. The gipsies had no other choice than to work in their traditional trades as shearers, butchers, smiths, horse-traders, tinkers, basket-makers etc., or to beg.

The continual persecution of the gipsies and the intolerance by the *payos* – which still exists today – led to a deeply rooted mistrust of every non-gipsy. The unwritten rule of the *gitanos*: "Don't mix with the payos, only to tell them lies or to rob them" dates back to that time.

A peculiar and proud way of singing and dancing developed in today's famous quarters, the former gitanerías of Sevilla (Triana), San Fernando (Cádiz) and Trinidad (Málaga) or on the Sacro Monte (Granada). Living in total isolation, only in touch with the poor with whom they shared their misery and sorrows, the *gitanos* developed Flamenco, a deep expression of desperation and hunger, from the music they had brought with them.

"Camelamos naquerar" ("we want to speak") was the title of a production of the "Teatro Gitano Andaluz" by MARIO MAYA in the 70s. To speak – not to fight! The *gitanos* have never revolted, never fought for their rights, never really resisted. When they met with hate, they responded with their own weapons: they had their families, their arrogance, indifference and contempt for those who harmed them – and they had their singing and their music. In this respect, nothing has changed. Nor has their social status changed. It's true there are some wealthy families or Flamenco artists or bull-fighters, but the majority of gipsies still lives in conditions inconceivable to us.

All those years I spent in a small town on the Costa del Sol, a town owing its prosperity to tourism, I came across begging *gitanas* in the streets every day. None of my Andalusian friends talked about them, none of them knew where they came from. It was just nothing worth talking about. The *gitanos* were there, and they were begging. Period! One day I was looking for a street on the outskirts of the town and found myself in a dead end. When I looked around I was not scared, but so surprised that I didn't find the reverse gear. Here, three kilometres from the bustle of the high-society tourists, complete with an unparalleled marina, people had to live in tin shacks! The majority of the people living in the slums, which can be found in other towns as well, are unemployed and illiterate. It is disconcerting that people don't talk about it, and that many Spanish people don't seem to know about the existence of the slums. After all, they have great advertisement like Triana or the Sacro Monte, where the gipsies live in "nice and romantic caves" and where "original, authentic Flamenco shows" with "pure-blooded Spanish women," clad in colourful dresses, are staged every night.

Terms

Cante andaluz, cante gitano, cante flamenco, cante jondo, cante gitano andaluz, arte andaluz, arte gitano, arte flamenco etc.: all these terms can be found in Flamenco literature. Still, Flamenco cannot be called folk music in the classic sense of the word. It would be better to call it "folk art"[13], because it cannot be properly performed by non-professionals in its original style without problems.

---

13 Marius Schneider, musicologist

It's true that Andalusia is called the cradle of Flamenco, but there are other songs from that region, such as the **Campanilleros,** the **Villancicos** and the majority of the **Sevillanas,** which, strictly speaking, do not belong to Flamenco. To limit Flamenco to Andalusia would be unjust to the "cantes flamencos de la periferia andaluza," *cantes* from adjoining regions, such as **Jaleos** and **Tangos** extremeños (extremadura), Cartagenas and **Murcianas** *(cante de levante)* from **Cartagena** and Murcia.

It would be wrong to call Flamenco the art of the gipsies. They had long been the only Flamenco performers and are still great Flamenco artists. Nobody denies that the gipsies have greatly influenced and perfected Flamenco, but they didn't create it. This is not proven alone by the fact that non-Spanish gipsies know nothing about Flamenco.

The adjective *jondo* is mostly used in connection with *cante,* but only the older vocal forms are assigned to this category. Moreover, it is up to the performer to sing, dance or play jondo. The word is often spelled hondo, because the Andalusians don't pronounce the "j" in a guttural way, but similar to the English "h." Another theory is that the word comes from the castellano word hondo (deep). However, if it is really derived from "deep," it will depend on the performance whether or not a cante is jondo. In this case, **Bulerías** may also be performed with "hondura" (depth). Others are of the opinion that jondo is derived from the Hebrew word "jom-tob" or "jom-tow." Some synagogue chants end on this word which means "good day."

The terms *grande* and *chico* refer to the degree of difficulty of a *cante.* The term intermedio, denoting anything between *jondo, grande* and *chico,* is rarely used.

At last, there is no choice but to use the term Flamenco. It is the most common term anyway. Cante flamenco, baile flamenco, toque flamenco, traje flamenco, cuadro flamenco, guitarra flamenca – I could carry on ad infinitum. However, the term "Flamenco" is also used for persons involved in Flamenco – and as an adjective. "Not everybody who plays Flamenco plays flamenco," GERARDO NUÑEZ once said in an interview[14]. Another example: I was wearing a white shirt with black spots once, which a singer *(gitana)* described as "muy flamenco!" Furthermore, "flamenco" is a special way of life, a special way of singing, playing dancing or doing something.

However, "flamenco" also means "Flemish." So, "arte flamenco" can also mean "Flemish art." If you look up "flamenco" in a dictionary, you will find 1. "flamingo" and 2. "Flemish," "gipsy-like," "gipsy". When CARLOS I (Charles V) became King of Spain, both his Flemish advisers and the ordinary soldiers from Flanders who were stationed in Spain, were allegedly very arrogant and boastful because the King's birthplace was Gent. The term "flamenco" as a synonym for "arrogant" or "proud" presumably dates from that time. Anyone who was proud and snooty, especially the gipsies, was called "flamenco." Some people even seriously supported the idea that the posture of the Flamenco dancers resembled that of the bird of the same name. And here is one last theory: there are similar-sounding Arabic and Moroccan words from which "Flamenco" could have been derived: "felaga menu" (fellahs = rural farming population of Syria, Palestine, Arabia and Algeria), "felah mangu" (Moroccan chant of the farmers), "felahikum" (Arabic chant of the farmers).

Development of Flamenco

As I already mentioned, Flamenco is the result of different ethnic elements, blending in the melting pot of Andalusia. If we date the actual beginning of Flamenco back to the Middle Ages, i.e. to the time when the music and songs brought to Spain by the gipsies and Moors began to interact and blend, we can easily imagine that these

---

Beautiful voice, carrying voice, many octaves, pure tones: all this applies to drawing-room music, operas and concertos, but not to Flamenco. The only thing that counts in Flamenco is passion – the excitement radiating from the singer, dancer and guitarist, pouring over the audience like burning phosphorus.
Juan Fernández "Talegas" (1887-1971)

From an interview with Juan Talegas by Carlos D. Obers in 1970.

"... los pajaritos y yo nos levantamos a un tiempo: ellos para cantar el alba, yo a llorar mi sentimiento ..."
"... the little birds and I get up at the same time: they get up to sing the praises of daybreak, and I, to cry out my feelings... ."

Paquera de Jerez

---

14 Anja Vollhardt, Flamenco – Kunst zwischen gestern und morgen

HISTORY

> Peno men ducas guillabando
> sos guillabar sina orobar.
> Peno retejos quelarando
> sos quelarar sina guirrar.
>
> I express my sorrow by singing
> because singing is crying.
> I express my joy by dancing
> because dancing is laughing.

Caló-lyrics by José Carlos de Luna, Los Gitanos de la Bética; loosely translated by Heike Brühl.

fringe groups, but especially the gipsies, cultivated and developed Flamenco as an outlet for their distress and desperation. RICARDO MOLINA said, "Flamenco is the elemental scream of a people that has sunk into poverty and ignorance. For this people, only primary needs and instinctive emotions exist. Their singing is desperation, discouragement, lament, mistrust, superstition, curse, magic, a wounded soul, a dark confession of a suffering and oppressed race. Singing is self-therapy. It is tragedy. No disguise, no playacting to impress the audience."

Before Flamenco was emerged in public, it had only been performed in front of the family or close friends. Everyone took an active part in those so-called *juergas,* singing, dancing, playing the guitar, *palmas* and *jaleos,* or at least by listening actively. Only in this circle of like-minded people, or people living under the same conditions, could the true spirit of Flamenco, the moment of truth, of ecstasy, the much quoted duende, unfold. One should be careful with the term duende, however, because the gitanos don't understand it at all if a payo talks about it. JUAN TALEGAS said about this subject, "Nonsense. Who put the idea of duende into the heads of you foreigners? Don't tell me it was GARCÍA LORCA! *Duende* is like a fever, like malaria. I only had *duende* twice in my life. Afterwards I had to be carried from the site." [15]

We don't know anything about the development of Flamenco prior to the 18th century. The period from 1800 to 1860 is regarded as the first known epoch in the existence of the art of Flamenco. This period is called *la época primitiva* or *la época primera.* Around 1850 the "white" Andalusian population began to develop an interest in Flamenco. The "señoritos" (sons of wealthy landowners) organised private *juergas* and didn't mind spending quite a bit of money on them. For the first time, Flamenco artists who had previously sung, played and danced only among their own kind and without an audience, were paid for their performances. In this first epoch of Flamenco singing, many singers accompanied themselves on the guitar. MOLINA/MAIRENA listed thirty-four creators and *cantaores* of the **Siguiriya** from that period. One of them isn't a gipsy: SILVERIO FRANCONETTI. It was he who brought Flamenco into the *cafés cantantes* and who later opened the famous "Café de Silverio" in Sevilla.

The era of the *cafés cantantes* is regarded as the second epoch of Flamenco. It began in Sevilla where the first *cafés* were opened in 1842. Soon, these *cafés,* where singers and guitarists could work professionally, were found not only in Andalusia, but in every major city, including Madrid. What was new, especially to the gitanos from whose ranks the majority of *cantaores* were recruited, was that they were expected to perform their Flamenco expressively on command, i.e. when the show began. Eventually, the whole thing turned into a routine, and the number of guests in the *cafés* began to drop considerably. During that time, Flamenco dance came to the fore and gradually acquired the same standing

---

15 Interview with Juan Fernández Talegas by Carlos D. Obers, 1970 (Flamenco-Mitteilungsblatt)

as the *cante*. The guitar, too, became an important part of Flamenco and began to develop into a solo instrument (see **Volume I**, Guitarristas). This epoch lasted until about 1910, followed by the decline of the *cafés* and a time which Flamenco artists don't care to remember. Flamenco was performed on the theatre stages, and a strange development began, culminating in the "Opera Flamenca," an absolute sentimentalization of Flamenco. There were Flamenco performances in revues and variety shows. The quality left a great deal to be desired because the audience, who liked light entertainment, decided what was to be en vogue. Even great artists such as JUAN BREVA and ENRIQUE EL MELLIZO, who were regarded as initiators, and ANTONIO CHACÓN, LA NIÑA DE LOS PEINES or MANUEL TORRE, had no choice but to join in these "espectáculos." Flamenco performances at the "corridas" (bull fights) were very popular, too. This era – also called "operismo" – was a bad time for Flamenco and ended with the beginning of the Civil War in 1936. A hard time began for the artists who had at least found work during the "operismo," because now cultural life came to a standstill.

Flamenco in the 1950s and Today

It was only in the fifties that Flamenco life changed again. The course of Flamenco was determined by several events: 1. the sound recording of the "Antalogía del Cante Flamenco" by Hispavox in 1954, compiled and arranged by PERICO DE CÁDIZ, EL GALLINA, JARRITO, BERNARDO EL DE LOS LOBITOS, EL CHAQUIETA, NIÑO DE MÁLAGA AND LOLITA TRIANA; 2. the development of the *tablaos,* which continued the heritage of the old *cafés cantantes.* The best known *tablao* was the "Zambra," followed by "El Corral de la Morería," "El Duende," "Torres Bermejas," " Café de Chinitas" and "Las Cuevas de Nemesio;" 3. the first "Concurso Nacional de Cante Jondo" in Córdoba in 1956. This event led to a stronger presence of the art of Flamenco in the media. Moreover, the competition influenced the development of the "Festivals de Cante" in Andalusia, similar to the competition in 1922 in Granada; 4. the bibliography material on Flamenco increased tremendously. Among the editors of books and articles were ANSELMO GONZÁLES CLIMENT, RAFAEL LAFUENTE, RICARDO MOLINA, DOMINGO MANFREDI, the Pakistani diplomat AZIZ BALOUCH, RAFAEL MANZANO, etc. The "Cátedra de Flamencología" and the "Estudios Folkloricos Andaluces," founded in 1958 by a group of poets from Jerez, can be regarded as additional milestones.

In the last two decades, artists have been trying to find ways of reviving Flamenco. Big events and joint projects such as the "Cumbre Flamenca" and "Los Veranos de la Villa" in Madrid and the "Bienal de arte Flamenco Ciudad de Sevilla" have been organised, not forgetting the opening of the Flamenco centre "Fundación Andaluza de Flamenco" in Jerez in 1988. The centre offers everything from Flamenco events to a museum, from a library and video library to an annual publication of the calendar of Flamenco events called "Anuario Flamenco y Guía de Festivales."

Los Tablaos

There are one or more *tablaos* in every major city today. Some of them have fallen into disrepute, especially in the touristy places, where the most important thing seems to be that good-looking gitanas are sitting on the stage and that their "volantes" are flying. However, you will find good artists in most of the famous tablaos in the big cities. In this context I would also like to mention that this way of performing Flamenco is necessary and justified. On the one hand, the tablaos offer many *profesionales* the chance to survive and many young artists the opportunity to develop their abilities further. On the other hand, it is often the only opportunity for people (tourists) to experience Flamenco "live" and to come into contact, however superficial, with the subject. Incidentally, the *tablao* is the best school for Flamenco artists. Purists totally dis-

> "Flamenco has two sources, joy and sadness. Body and soul must be in harmony. You need intelligence to guide the body when dancing, or the voice when singing, and you need heart to get the meaning across."

Pepe el de la Matrona (cantaor)

approve of this development and performance in the *tablao*. They need to consider, however, that the original Flamenco no longer exists, at least not in public. This may be regrettable, but then again, I am glad that this kind of Flamenco exists as well, otherwise many people, including myself, wouldn't have been able to join Flamenco.

El Cante – El Baile – El Toque

Authentic Flamenco is intuitive ensemble playing, with the *cante* as the most important element. While the *cantaor* is singing, the guitar must follow him and provide the harmonic background. The *tocaor* can play his *falsetas* between the *letras* or, better, between the *coplás*. In Flamenco dance, too, the guitar functions only as an accompanying instrument. An elaborate accompaniment of cante and *baile* requires a lot of intuition and sensitivity on the part of the *tocaor*, and must be regarded just as highly as the virtuoso *falsetas* played by a solo guitarist. Spontaneity is an important characteristic of Flamenco. Without it, Flamenco would sound sterile and stiffly unnatural and would thus be inconsistent with the lifestyle of the *flamencos*. What I am trying to tell the guitarist is that it is not enough to rehearse *falsetas*. The best thing to do is to find a job, as quickly as possible, at a dancing school where Flamenco is taught. There are Flamenco dancing schools in every major city today. The teachers are always grateful if they have a guitarist, and you'll learn a lot.

Pasión

What a great, stimulating form of art Andalucía has brought forth: an art deeply rooted in the soul of its people. An elemental musical culture has developed on Europe's border, reflecting the spirit and identity of a whole nation. This culture could only develop because of the mixture of pride and poverty, enabling the Andalusians, like almost no other people, to express their suffering so intensely, to do without many material things, and in return allow themselves what is almost forbidden in our affluent society: pasión.

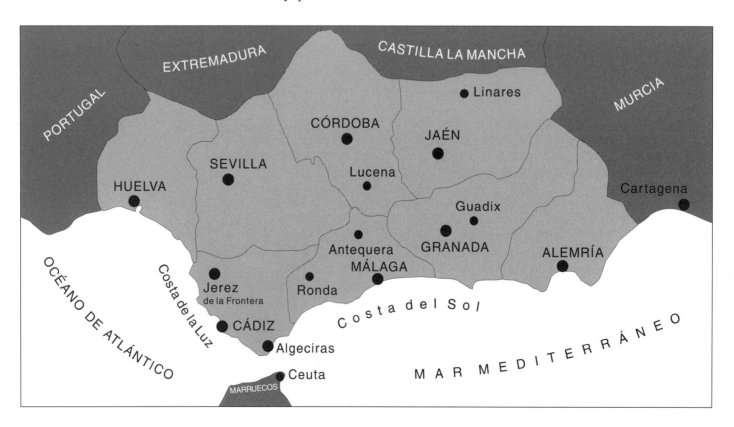

Bibliography

Almendros, Carlos: Todo lo básico sobre el Flamenco, Barcelona 1973

Alvarez Caballero, Angel: Historia del Cante Flamenco, Madrid 1981 / Gitanos, Payos y Flamencos, En los Orígenes del Flamenco, Madrid 1988

Batista, Andrés: Manual Flamenco, Madrid 1985

Blas Vega, José: Los cafés Cantantes de Sevilla, Madrid 1987

Blas Vega, José y Rios Ruiz, Manuel: Diccionario Flamenco I + II, Madrid 1988

Caballero Bonald, José Maria: Archivo del Cante Flamenco, Barcelona 1969

Camacho, Galindo: Los Payos tambien cantan Flamenco, Madrid 1977

Clébert, Jean-Paul: Los Gitanos, Barcelona 1965

Diaz-Plaja, Fernando: Spanien, Nyon 1976

Falla, Manuel de: Escritos sobre música y músicas, Madrid 1972

García Lorca, Federico: Obras completas, Madrid 1973

Gelardo, José y Belade, Francine: Socieadad y Cante Flamenco, Madrid 1985

Gonzales Climent, Anselmo: Flamencología, Madrid 1964

George, David: The Flamenco Guitar, Madrid 1969

Grande, Felix: Memoria del Flamenco, Madrid 1979

Mairena, Antonio: Las confesiones de Antonio Mairena, Sevilla 1976

Martinez de la Peña, Teresa: Teoría y Prática del Baile Flamenco, Madrid 1969

Mauritz, Walter: El Arte Flamenco, »Flamenco« 2 - 4, Geiselbach 1983 (Eberwein)

Molina, Ricardo y Mairena, Antonio: Mundo y formas del Cante Flamenco, Granada/Sevilla 1971

Münster, Thomas: Zigeuner-Saga, Freiburg 1969

Obers, Carlos D.: Drei alte Männer, Flamenco-Mitteilungsblatt 7, Mainz 1972

Pohren, D. E.: The Art of Flamenco, Madrid 1990 / Lives and Legend, Madrid 1988 / A way of Life, Madrid 1980

Pohren, D. E.: Paco de Lucía, Madrid 1993

Puig Claramunt, Alfonso/Albaicín, Flora: El Arte del Baile Flamenco, Barcelona 1977

Reinhard, Michael D.: Mitteilungen zur Zigeunerkunde / Wortliste des Dialekts der spanischen Zigeuner, Flamencostudio Mainz

Renner, Hans: Geschichte der Musik, Stuttgart 1965

Rioja, Eusebio y Cañete, Angel Luis: La Guitarra Flamenca, Sesión de Estudio de la Peña Juan Breva, Málaga 1986

Robert, René: Flamencos, Paris 1993

Sing, Hansjörg: Andalusien, Kunst- und Reiseführer, Ulm 1988

Stolzenberg, Elke/Alvarez Caballero, Angel: Las Mascaras de lo Jondo, Madrid 1993

Thiel-Cramér, Barbara: Flamenco, Lindingö (Schweden) 1991

Triana, Fernando el de: Arte y Artistas Flamencos, Madrid 1935

Vian, Cesno: Spanien, Brücke zwischen Abendland und Orient, Stuttgart 1991

Villar Rodríguez, José: La Guitarra Española, Barcelona 1985

Vollhardt, Anja/Stolzenberg, Elke: Flamenco, Weingarten 1988

Epilogue

Actually, there is much more to write about Flamenco. Moreover, many more "estilos" and "palos" should have been treated in both volumes. Trying to achieve this target would be a futile undertaking, though, because Flamenco, with its past and present, is an inexhaustable subject. Anyone who would like to study it in greater detail may read some of the books listed in the bibliography. There are also more music and tablature editions than you would think. Furthermore, there are many good Flamenco guitarists who also teach Flamenco guitar.

Writing these two Volumes took me much longer than I had ever expected. Sometimes the complexity of the subject of Flamenco nearly drove me to despair. That is why I would like to thank all those who supported me, directly or indirectly, in starting, realising and finishing this project: first and foremost my wife, Lela de Fuenteprado, and my son Marco, as well as Andrés Batista (Madrid), my students and my editor, who did not only do the proof-reading, but who also immersed himself in the subject and inspired me with many ideas.

Lela de Fuenteprado and José Fortes — Photo: Claudia Ammann

CD-Tracks

Nr	Title	Time
01	Sencillos I (Tangos)	0:14
02	3-Finger-Rasgueo	0:08
03	Estudio por Soleá	0:25
04	4-Finger-Rasgueo	0:10
05	Sencillos II (Tangos)	1:10
06	Naino I (Tangos)	0:37
07	Naino II (Tangos)	1:12
08	Naino III (Tangos)	0:38
09	Naino IV (Tangos)	0:55
10	Mantón I (Soleá)	0:41
11	Caí I (Alegrías en Do)	0:36
12	Ayudado Exercise I	0:36
13	Ayudado Exercise II	0:16
14	Rumbita I (Rumba)	0:45
15	Mantón II (Soleá)	1:14
16	i-downstroke with Golpe	0:22
17	p-downstroke with Golpe	0:23
18	Naino V (Tangos)	3:06
19	Quejío (Taranto)	2:27
20	Rumba-Compás I	0:28
21	Rumba-Compás II	0:27
22	Rumba-Compás III	0:28
23	Rumba-Compás IV	0:28
24	Rumba-Compás V	0:30
25	Rumba-Compás VI	0:28
26	Tangos-Compás with Tresillos I	0:46
27	Soleá-Compás with Tresillos I	0:20
28	Soleá-Compás with Tresillos II	0:20
29	Soleá-Compás with Tresillos III	0:21
30	Soleá-Compás with Tresillos IV	0:20
31	Fandango de Huelva	0:43
32	Sevillanas	0:57
33	Paso Lento (Alegría)	1:00
34	Mantón III (Soleá)	1:50
35	Quejío II (Taranto)	1:46
36	Mantón IV (Soleá)	0:42
37	Mantón V (Soleá)	1:03
38	Mantón VI (Soleá)	1:07
39	Rumbita II (Rumba)	1:31
40	Tremolo Exercise I	0:27
41	Tremolo Exercise II	0:25
42	Quejío III (Taranto)	2:09
43	Lérida (Garrotín)	2:49
44	Palo Seco I (Bulerías Exercise)	0:08
45	Palo Seco II (Bulerías Exercise)	0:08
46	Palo Seco III (Bulerías Exercise)	0:08
47	Palo Seco IV (Bulerías Exercise)	0:08
48	Bulerías-Compás I	0:19
49	Bulerías-Compás II	0:18
50	Bulerías-Compás III	0:19
51	Bulerías-Compás IV	0:19
52	Bulerías-Compás V	0:19
53	Bulerías-Compás VI	0:19
54	Bulerías-Compás VII	0:19
55	Bulerías-Compás VIII	0:19
56	Bulerías-Compás IX	0:19
57	Bulerías-Compás X	0:19
58	Bulerías-Compás XI	0:19
59	Bulerías-Compás XII	0:20
60	Bulerías-Compás XIII	0:20
61	Bulerías-Compás XIV	0:19
62	Bulerías-Compás XV	0:20
63	Bulerías-Compás XVI	0:19
64	Bulerías-Compás XVII	0:19
65	Bulerías-Compás XVIII	0:28
66	Columpio I (Bulerías)	0:57
67	Columpio II (Bulerías)	0:58
68	Columpio III (Bulerías)	0:58
69	Alzapúa I (Exercise)	0:28
70	Alzapúa II (Exercise)	0:17
71	Alzapúa III (Exercise)	0:17
72	Alzapúa IV (Exercise)	1:33
73	Alzapúa V (Exercise)	0:32
74	Alzapúa VI (Exercise)	0:32
75	Mantón VII (Soleá)	0:25
76	Mantón VIII (Soleá)	0:36
77	Mantón IX (Soleá)	0:44
78	Mantón X (Soleá)	0:49
79	Alegría en Mi I (Compás Exercise)	0:59
80	Alegría en Mi II (Compás Exercise)	1:00
81	Alegría en Mi III (Intro)	1:02
82	Alegría en Mi IV (Escobilla)	1:02
83	Alegría en Mi V (Puente)	0:59
84	Caí II (Alegría en Do)	0:56
85	Caí III (Alegría en Do)	1:26
86	Caí IV (Alegría en Do)	1:00
87	Caí V (Alegría en Do)	1:05
88	Columpio IV (Bulerías)	4:02
89	Columpio V (Bulerías)	0:58
90	Quejío IV (Taranto)	2:40
91	Naino VI (Tangos)	2:13
92	Naino VII (Tangos)	0:54
93	Naino VIII (Tangos)	0:38

Index

A

Al-Andalus	118-119
Alegrías	70
Almohades	19, 121
Almoravides	119
Alzapúa	57
Arabs	118
Arpegio	9
a-Arpegio	11
p-i-m-a-Arpegio	32
Triplets	11
Arte	
Andaluz	124
flamenco	125
Autodafés	121
Aztecs	122

B

Berber	118
Bulerías	
por arriba	39
Bulerías I	39
Bulerías II	81

C

Café Cantante	126
Cante	
andaluz	124
chico	125
de la periferia andaluza	125
extremeños	125
grande	125
hondo	125
intermedio	125
jondo	125
cantes	
de abandolaos	100
de los Zíngaros	103
Carthaginians	117
Catholicism	121
Cave paintings	115
Celtiberians	117
Celts	117
cierre	42, 48

INDEX

compás alterno 42
Conquista 120, 122
Conquistadores 122
contras 40
Conversos 121
corridas 127
Crwth 115
Cultura Almeriense 115

D

desarrollo 50
Duende 126

E

Egipciano 123
Esfandangos 99
Estilos 95
Etruscans 116

F

Felaga menu 125
Felah mangu 125
Felahikum 125
Fellahs 125
Flamenco mode 31
Flamenco clock 39
Flamencos 125
Flanders 125
Folk art 124
Foot 39

G

Gades 117
Gadir 116
Gipsy 123
Gitane 123
Gitanerías 123
Gitanos 123, 126
Greeks 116

H

Hispania 117
horquilla .... 45 - 46

I

Iberians 115
Iberia 117
Inkas 122

Inquisition 121, 123

J

jaleo 39
Yemenis 118
Jom-tob 125
Jews . . . . 116, 119 - 120
Juergas 126

K

Kinnor 116
Kol-Nidre region 121

L

Laúd 119
Ligurians 116

M

Miralles 115
Modo dórico 31, 115
   see also Volume I, Glossary
Moors . . . . 118, 120 - 121
Moriscos 121
Moros 118
Murgas 108

N

Nasrids 120

O

Omaijades 119, 121
Opera flamenca 127
Operismo 127

P

palmas 39
Payos 124
Picado 29
pie 41
Phoenicians 116
pregunta 50

R

Reconquista 120
reloj 39
remate 68, 71
respuesta 50, 68
Reyes Católicos . . . . 120 -121, 123

Romance 119
romaní 122
Romans 117

S

Sacro Monte 124
Saetas 121
Santa Fé 120
Sefardís 121
Seguidillas 96
   Castellanas 102
   Manchegas 106
Seguirillas Andaluzas 102
Señoritos 126
Sepharad 120
Sephardim 120
Siglo de Oro 122
Soleá 65
Synagogue chants 125
Syrians 118

T

taifas 119
Tartessos . . . . .116 -117
temple 48
Tonada 109
Tremolo 22
Tyrrhenians 116

V

Vandals 117
Vibrato 50
Visigoths 118

Z

Zambra 111
Zángano 109